Common Sense
FAMILIES

Dr. Roy W. Harris

Common Sense FAMILIES

This book was printed in the United States of America.

To order additional copies of this book contact::

Dr. Roy W. Harris
906 Castle Heights Ave.
Lebanon, Tennessee 37087
roy@royharris.info
615-351-1425

Order Online
@
www.amazon.com

RHM
Publications

SPECIAL THANKS To:

Amy D. Harris, for her love, support, help and encouragement with this project and my entire ministry.

Missy and **Aaron** my wonderful children, (and their spouses Tim and Susan) for the wonderful young adults and excellent parents they have become.

Marissa, Mason, Claire, Lauren and Rachel my grandchildren who bring Pawpaw and Mimi such joy and pleasure. (Each one is my favorite.)

Diana L. Harris who helped me as a young man, learn about marriage, life and raising Godly children to serve the Lord.

Dr. Jack Williams my writing mentor, encourager, and editor.

Roy Harris Ministries

Table of Contents

Introduction

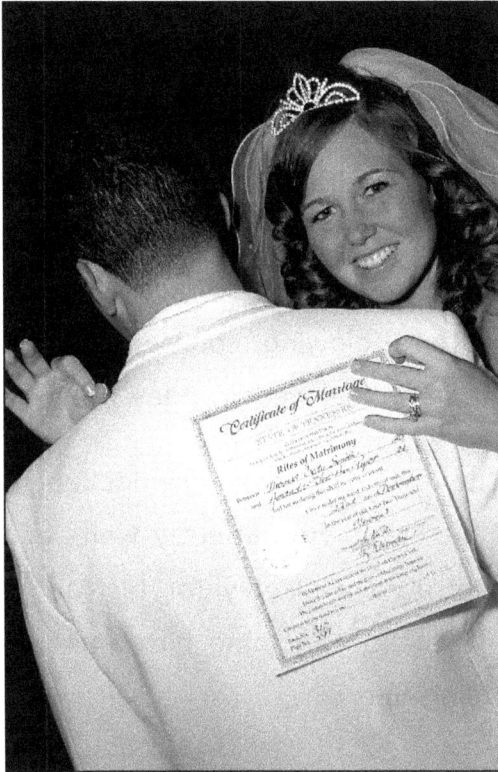

Thomas and Amanda, a fine young couple Roy counseled and married.

The big day finally arrives! The audience rises with the command of the minister and slowly all eyes focus on the doors at the rear of the auditorium.

The musicians strike up the nostalgic song that beckons arrival of the bride.

The beautifully adorned bride appears like an angel in the doorway. Her carefully chosen white gown, veiled face, and sculptured hair create a glowing countenance that that only a bride on her wedding day possesses.

The groom's eyes are locked with the eyes of his bride. He patiently waits at the end of the betrothal walkway for his lady to glide the short distance, joining him and the rest of the wedding party.

He is dressed in the finest attire he has ever worn complete with silk shirt, bowtie, and patent leather shoes.

The couple vows to stick together, through thick and thin come what may, so long as they both shall live. Their two lives have now become one full of joy, happiness, and hope for a wonderful long life together.

Fast-forward a few years to a different scene. The couple that couldn't wait to be alone together on their wedding day now find themselves not wanting to be in the same room together.

Some small incident brings the tumultuous relationship to a head. Lawyers are hired. The couple and their lawyers are seated at a conference table facing each other.

Papers have been prepared, terms established, and the divorce settlement has been agreed upon. The couple is about to sign the official documents that will dissolve their marriage, assign custody and visitation rights for their children, and divide their belongings.

Let's shift to another scene in a local hospital with another couple. Months have passed since the young couple first received the news that a little one would be joining their family.

The labor pains began hours ago. Husband and wife are now about to become mom and dad. They experience the wonderful miracle of birth together. Seeing, touching, holding, smelling this wonderful gift from God has forever changed their lives.

They bring the infant home and the challenge and experience of child rearing has begun. For the next 18 years major portions of finance and focus will be on this child as he grows up in their home.

The child has been such a joy to have in their home for the past 12 years or so. Almost overnight the parents notice a big change in the personality and attitude of their soon-to-be teenage child. They never dreamed he could be this way and life could be so hard.

The phone rings and it's the child's principal. The poor grades and progress reports have arrived like clockwork from the child's teachers for some time. Now the principal says the child has become a discipline problem at school.

What is a parent to do? Where did they go wrong? What can they do now?

Unfortunately, the two descriptions mentioned above along with some others that could've been mentioned, are common in our 21st century culture. Almost half of all marriages will end up in divorce. Statistics show that children who grow up in Christian homes fall into some of the same dependency and discipline traps as those who do not.

There is hope for our marriages and our children. The Bible, the greatest book of wisdom and guidance ever written, defines relationships, roles, responsibilities, and rewards for marriages and raising children.

The purpose of this book is to provide practical *common sense* principles that will strengthen marriages, build up children and create the environment in homes where parents and children build enduring lifelong relationships by understanding who God is and how He can help them.

The practical suggestions offered in this book are based on Biblical principles, 40 years of successful marital experience, counseling countless married couples, working closely as a college dean with hundreds of college students, pastoring hundreds of families, raising my two children and now the proud pawpaw of five wonderful grandchildren.

Good marriages do not happen by accident; they require hard work. Raising children to honor and respect their parents and give proper place to God and His Word requires constant and consistent efforts by parents.

There are no perfect marriages, perfect parents, or perfect children. But there are powerful common sense principles built upon the foundation of the Word of God that can help imperfect people perfect the art of becoming good parents, and raising good children.

Read this book with an open mind understanding that it does not have all the answers. Every situation is different because people and families are different. Ask God to help you glean from the book things that will instruct, encourage, and help you work to make your house a home.

Chapter 1

Love Me Tender, Love Me True

Aaron, Roy's son was asked to impersonate Elvis at the McAlister's 50th wedding anniversary party. (He was good)

2 Corinthians 9:6-9

But I say this, He who sows sparingly shall also reap sparingly, and he who sows bountifully shall also reap bountifully. Each one, as he purposes in his heart, let him give; not of grief, or of necessity, for God loves a cheerful giver. And God is able to make all grace abound toward you, that in everything, always having all self-sufficiency, you may abound to every good work; As it is written, "He scattered; he has given to the poor; his righteousness remains forever.

One night, a man decided to show his wife how much he loved her.

After dinner he began reciting romantic poetry, telling her he would climb high mountains to be near her, swim wide oceans, cross deserts in the burning heat of day, and sit at her window and sing love songs to her in the moonlight.

After listening to him go on for some time about this immense love he had, she ended the conversation by asking him one question. At the end of the chapter you will find out what she asked and his answer.

Why do the euphoria and excitement of dating and the wonderful first days of marital bliss soon dissipate, only to end a few years later in divorce? Over half of those who say *I DO* eventually decide *I DON'T* anymore. What happens? Why doesn't it last?

Engaged couples approach marriage with a number of preconceptions. They mistakenly think the person they are about to marry is almost perfect. They believe they understand what the other person is thinking. They believe their mate's needs are basically identical to their own.

Once married, the newness of the physical relationship soon is trumped by the reality of daily responsibilities and the normal ups and downs of life. Those first months and years of marriages are so important. Those early days establish patterns and courses of action that will help marriages grow and flourish or doom them to eventual failure.

Love is like adolescent children who must live, learn, and grow into mature adults. I was four months past my 19th birthday when I moved from the ranks of bachelorhood to the roles of marital bliss.

I didn't know much about marriage, well; I really didn't know anything about marriage. I just knew I loved that pretty, dark-haired, blue-eyed beauty.

It didn't take long for me to realize how different we were. I must confess it was a little bumpy early on. We entered into marriage as most couples do, not really having a clue of what marriage was all about.

Diana, Roy's first wife who later died of breast cancer.

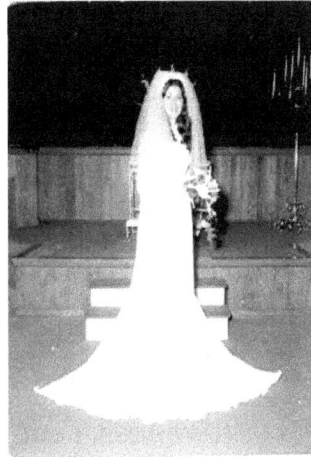

One thing we learned quickly. Marriage was work, hard work. We both had grown up in homes where work was exalted as a virtue and hard work was expected.

We knew we loved each other and wanted to spend our lives together. We began what was to become 33 years of married life learning. Through the years we began and continued to discover how the other was different.

We discovered what the other person needed from our relationship and in turn, how we could seek to address and meet those needs. We discovered when the goal of each was to meet the needs of the other; our own needs were met also.

One of the biggest things I learned through the whole process was how being different was truly an asset to our marriage. Our differences kept it interesting, even when they sparked disagreements.

Love is a feeling.

Love is a feeling but much more than just a feeling. Love is a mental attitude that carries the day through times of illness, financial setbacks, disappointments, discouragement, and heartaches. Difficult circumstances provide fertile soil from which love may be enhanced and grow.

The Christian can choose to love anything. He will cherish the object of his love and do whatever is necessary to provide for the needs of the object of his affections.

Love is finding a plan.

The greatest object of our love should be Jesus Christ. It all begins with Him. If we are to learn how to love others, then we must look to the example already displayed for us. We do not have to guess what the Lord wants from us.

The *first thing* God wants from us is *obedience* to His instructions according to John 14:21;

> *He who has My commandments and keeps them, he it is who loves Me. And he who loves Me shall be loved by My Father, and I will love him and*

will reveal Myself to him.

If we are to love others we must know how. We can know how by learning, listening to, and living out God's instructions for us.

A *second thing* God wants from us is *worship, praise, and appreciation* of Him according to Psalm 107:8

> *Oh that men would praise Jehovah for his loving kindness, And for his wonderful works to the children of men!*

He wants us to worship Him for who He is. He wants us to praise Him for what He has done. He wants us to appreciate Him for what He is doing in, for, and through us.

A *third thing* God wants from us is to *enjoy fellowship* with us. He wants us to spend time with Him and place Him high on our priority list, according to John 1:7-9;

> *This one came as a witness, to bear witness concerning the Light, so that all might believe through him. He was not that Light, but was sent to bear witness of that Light. He was the true Light; He enlightens every man coming into the world.*

Love is following the instructions.

The Bible compares the relationship Christ has with His Church to that of a bride and groom, Ephesians 5:21- 33:

Subjecting yourselves one to another in the fear of Christ. Wives, be in subjection unto your own husbands, as unto the Lord. For the husband is the head of the wife, as Christ also is the head of the church, being himself the savior of the body. But as the church is subject to Christ, so let the wives also be to their husbands in everything. Husbands, love your wives, even as Christ also loved the church, and gave himself up for it; that he might sanctify it, having cleansed it by the washing of water with the word, that he might present the church to himself a glorious church, not having spot or wrinkle or any such thing; but that it should be holy and without blemish. Even so ought husbands also to love their own wives as their own bodies. He that loveth his own wife loveth himself: for no man ever hated his own flesh; but nourisheth and cherisheth it, even as Christ also the church; because we are members of his body. For this cause shall a man leave his father and mother, and shall cleave to his wife; and the two shall become one flesh. This mystery is great: but I speak in regard of Christ and of the church. Nevertheless do ye also severally love each one his own wife even as himself; and let the wife see that she fear her husband.

Christ is the groom and the Church the bride. The bride and groom complement each other. They are different by design. The Lord, the groom, provides some key elements in how husbands and wives should try to understand each other. We are to praise, appreciate, and spend time with each other. All those things are important.

Love is fulfilling needs.

God created men and women to complement each other. Men and women have different needs. Love is about meeting those needs. True love is embarking on a mission to discover the other person's needs. Discovering needs is the important first step toward the continual growth of love in marriage. The next huge step is committing to do whatever is humanly possible to meet those needs.

If a man and his wife are to experience the fulfillment of real love, they must learn "How to Love."

Later in the book we will look at the basic needs of men and women. By understanding these needs, Couples can learn "How to Love."

Love is giving

Unselfish giving has no thought of return. 2 Corinthians 9:6: *But I say this, He who sows sparingly shall also reap sparingly, and he who sows bountifully shall also reap bountifully*.

We must make up our minds to give ourselves without reservation.

2 Corinthians 9:7: *Each one, as he purposes in his heart, let him give; not of grief, or of necessity, for God loves a cheerful giver.*

God will help us know how to love our mates and without reserve.

2 Corinthians 9:8: *And God is able to make all grace abound toward you, that in everything, always having all self-sufficiency, you may abound to every good work.*

Back to our story........

One night, a man decided to show his wife how much he loved her.

After dinner he began to recite romantic poetry, telling her he would climb high mountains to be near her, swim wide oceans, cross deserts in the burning heat of day, and even sit at her window and sing love songs in the moonlight.

After listening to him go on for some time about this immense love he had, she ended the conversation when she asked, *"But will you do the dishes for me?"*

ACTION STEPS

1. What is love?

   _____

   _____

   _____

2. What does love require?

   _____

   _____

   _____

3. What have I gleaned from this chapter that will help me build a better marriage?

   _____

   _____

   _____

Chapter 2

The Woman of the House

The woman's role in the home is very important. The woman's touch and her fingerprints can be found throughout the house and imprinted on her husband and children.

Missy, Roy's daughter with Roy' grandson Mason.

Women bring femininity to the home. Women have the ability to see, feel and understand things that go right past men. Men were made with an empty spot in their hearts and lives that can only be filled by the presence of women.

Women not only bring many good things to the home, but God gives them specific responsibilities for their homes and families. No one else can fulfill the responsibilities designed for women by God.

Women often feel their roles are not important. But let me assure you that the lady of the house is the glue that holds the family together.

Women should seek to understand their roles and work hard to fulfill them. They must remind themselves of their roles and also respect the roles of their husbands. Marriages are doomed for serious trouble when the roles of the husbands and wives are not well defined and understood by both.

God designated the man of the house to be the head of the home. The husband will stand before God one day and answer to Him for the way he led his family. The woman's role is equally important and requires specific elements be present in order to be successful

1. Salvation through Jesus Christ is the first element the woman of the home should possess.

If women want to know God's plan for their families, then they must first know God personally. The lady who wishes to know her proper role in the home must be in a position to hear the voice of the Holy Spirit.

This begins with accepting Jesus Christ as her Savior and Lord. She comes to understand her role as she grows and matures as a Christian lady.

Women who do not know Christ can be caring, loving and dedicated to their families. But they will be spiritually handicapped and unable to be to their families the women God designed them to be.

Women who are sensitive to the voice of God and obedient to His instructions can become the wives and mothers they wish to be and God intends for them to be. Fervent faithful prayer and a hunger to know and understand the Word of God will help accomplish this.

Women who try to fix problems in their personal lives and the lives of their family members without knowing Christ are merely applying a Band-Aid to wounds that require the hand of the *Great Physician*.   In order to understand what God's will and plan is for the woman of the house, she must establish a personal relationship with Jesus Christ.

2. The second element that should be present in the woman's life is her personal commitment and dedication to the Lord.

What does it mean to be dedicated to the Lord? Dedication requires a total surrendering of one's life to Him. Nothing can be withheld and everything you are or ever will be is placed under His direction and control.

Everything one possesses or will possess has been pledged to Him and belongs to Him. One's time, talent, and treasure have been given to the Lord. Practically speaking, it requires faithful and total surrender to the service of the Lord.

The woman of the house must be consistent in her walk with the Lord. A good question to ask; how dedicated would my family say I am to the service of the Lord?

Families observe how we live and behave on a daily basis. Families know if the lady of the house is genuine and consistent in her Christian walk and life.

The family senses if the lady of the house is walking closely with the Lord or if she is not.   Evidence of her dedication will be exampled through her lifestyle. The Lord must come first, family second.

3. The lady of the house should pray for her husband and children. There is little doubt in most cases that the woman of the house loves her husband and children.

The greatest thing she can do for her family is spend time in prayer. Children and husbands will be impacted greatly by the prayers of a loving wife and mother. Going to our heavenly Father, as an advocate on behalf of our families is one of the greatest acts of love and service we can do for them.

4. A fourth element, which should be present in the woman of the house, is a concentrated effort to withhold criticism. Care should be taken when discussing serious matters or criticizing others in front of your children.

Criticizing pastors, Schoolteachers, Sunday school or Life Group leaders, family members, employees at work, etc. may influence your children's attitudes and behavior in a negative way.

Criticism may be warranted, but it should be done privately and out of earshot of the children. Criticism may result in unexpected consequences, wrong attitudes, and actions in our children.

5. A fifth element is the woman of the house must allow the man to be the man of the house. Honoring God's plan of placing the man in the position of leader in the home is essential for the home to be successful. Respect for the position of the man of the house is not always easy for the wife.

Husbands and wives both have important roles. Why? Because we are instructed in what the proper order of the home should be in God's holy Word.

6. Women and men should not criticize or correct their mates in public. Interrupting

one's mate in midsentence is rude and shows disrespect. Even if the spouse is incorrect in their account or information. Care should be taken in how correction enters into the conversation.

7. Women should be thankful and proud of the men they married. He may not be all you thought he would be or the perfect man you imagined, but he is *your man*. God gave him to you.

Do not constantly be comparing your husband to other men. Your husband may have his faults but other men do also. You may think you could have done better, but when you honestly think about it, you could have done much worse.

8. Women should take note of their husband's good points. There are many good things that should be remembered and recognized.

Women whose husbands are not Christians should be very careful about constantly confronting them over their faults and shortcomings. Making him feel inferior because he is not a Christian will have the effect of pushing him away from Christianity rather than drawing him closer to it.

9. The woman must allow the man to be the head disciplinarian in the home. There should be a measure of reverential fear instilled in children when it comes to the father. When Mom says; *just wait until your father gets home*, it should be the *big gun* that grabs the attention and affects the behavior of children.

10. Wives should be careful about disagreeing with their husband concerning discipline decisions in front of the children. Children test the waters early to see if they can pit one parent against the other, and they will use that tactic to get their way. This can become a point of contention between parents and hurt their relationship with each other.

Women who block their husbands from disciplining their children have opened the gates for much bigger problems with their children later in life. Failure to adequately deal with the small matters when they are young will plant bad seeds of behavior that will mature and be harvested when they become teenagers.

This does not mean that the father always makes the best decisions when it comes to disciplining children. The wife may perceive the discipline is too harsh or severe. It is not wrong for her to talk with her husband about his decision.

This should be done in private away from the children. They should not hear the discussion and the man should relay to the children any adjustments made to the decisions.

Major discipline decisions should be arrived at after discussions between the mother and father.

11. The wife should complement the husband's role as spiritual leader in the home providing the husband is a Christian. In many cases, the wife is more spiritually mature than the husband. Wives should be very careful to not upstage their husbands when they are putting forth a good effort to lead their families down spiritual paths.

12. Wives should allow husbands to be the final authority in making decisions in the home. Decision-making should be a cooperative effort between husbands and wives. Matters should be researched, evaluated, discussed between husbands and wives. Both should seek to understand and appreciate the other's viewpoint on the matter at hand. But in the end, only one person can make the decision.

13. Women should see problems in the home and make efforts to deal with them.

When women sense their husbands are under pressure and need to take some time to relax, encourage them to do it. Encourage them to spend a little money going hunting, fishing or playing a round of golf. Ladies should be sensitive to their husband's needs. More is said later in the book about this.

When wives sense their husbands are going through personal difficulties, they should find ways to get them to talk about it. Be careful confronting this head on. Men, many times do not feel like talking. The timing must be right, but they need to share. They will talk with their wives when they will not talk to anyone else.

When there is a breakdown in the relationship that cannot be mended, encourage the husband to go with you to seek help. There is nothing wrong with seeking help. Christian counselors can help spouses open closed doors and resolve conflicts in a biblical, God-honoring manner.

ACTION THOUGHTS

1. How important is the woman's role in the home?_____

_____

_____

_____

2. What are some areas in which I can improve in my role as woman of the house?

_____

_____

_____

_____

3. What important lesson(s) did I learn

from this chapter?

_____

_____

_____

_____

Chapter 3

My Wife the Queen

One day, three men were hiking and unexpectedly came upon a large, raging, violent river. They needed to get to the other side, but had no idea of

Roy's lovely bride Amy

how to do so. The first man prayed to God, saying, "Please God, give me the strength to cross this river."

POOF! God gave him big arms and strong legs, and he was able to swim across the river in about an hour, after almost drowning a couple of times.

Seeing this, the second man prayed to God, saying, "Please God, give me the strength and the tools to cross this river."

POOF! God gave him a rowboat and he was able to row across the river in about a half-hour, after almost capsizing the boat a couple of times.

The third man saw how this worked out for the other two, so he also prayed to God saying, "Please God, give me the strength and the tools...and the intelligence...to cross this river."

You may find it hard to believe what God did for this man. But you can find out at the end of this chapter.

If couples are to experience the fruits of real love in their marriage, they must learn how to love each other. Loving is about discovering and supplying the other person's needs.

Mates sometimes make the mistake of thinking that their mates want and need the same things they want and need. Nothing could be further from the truth. Just as husbands and wives differ physically, they also differ in what they need from their mates.

Two Basic Needs of Wives

The role of wives is wrapped up in two basic needs: Security and the need to be Homemakers. The wise husband will try to discover and understand his wife's needs and devote time, talent and treasure in efforts to meet those needs.

Security

Security, according to the Encarta Dictionary, is *the state or feeling of being safe and protected.* Wives must feel safe. They must know their husbands will protect them at all times and at all cost.

A husband's first loyalty is to his wife. That loyalty transcends loyalty to his parents, children, occupation, ministry or hobby. Wives must feel that they are number one with their husbands and that their position is secure.

How can men help their wives feel secure and protected? There are a number of things they can do.

First of all husbands should be consistently supportive. Wives need to be constantly reassured. They are concerned about their looks, their decisions, their mistakes, their cooking, their cleaning and you name it. Husbands should look for ways to compliment their wives. Complimenting their looks is especially important. Do not be critical! Men should look for ways to reassure them that they are beautiful and how proud of and thankful they are for them.

A second way husbands can make their wives feel secure is to be present and accounted for at crucial times. When there is a *bump in the night* in the house, the husband is the one who should say; *Honey, stay here and I'll check it out.*

Sleeping on the side of the bed closest to the door of the bedroom lets wives know husbands will be between them and potential danger. When walking with wives down the street or across the parking lot, men should stay between them and the traffic.

My wife knows I do things like this to always stay between her and danger. These are small gestures that send strong messages that you will always stand between her and danger. She will feel protected and safe.

49

Husbands should be present and accounted for when day-to-day problems arise. When the car needs repair, husbands should tell their wives that they will take care of getting the car repaired.

When the washing machine breaks down, husbands should take care of remedying the problem. Purchase a small toolbox with a few basic tools in it and keep it in the house. Screwdrivers, a pair of pliers, a small crescent wrench, and other small tools will come in handy for small household repairs.

Husbands should remember there is no time like the present to fix little things around the house. A loose cabinet hinge, a closet door that won't stay closed, a loose commode seat that could be tightened by hand in two minutes, a light bulb that needs changing can all be put off with good intentions of eventually getting round to fixing them.

Good intentions do not culminate in completed action. Husbands, you'll speak volumes to your wives and their worth by taking care of those little household things sooner rather than later.

Husbands should be the *big gun* wives can count on in handling problems with the children. The threat of *just wait until your dad gets home* provides the support wives and mothers need to reassure them that they have the strength of their husbands to lean on at crucial times.

A *third way* husbands can make their wives feel safe, secure, and protected is by spending time daily talking with their wives. Husbands must make time *every day* to talk with their wives. After dinner and before going to bed is a great time to do this.

Husbands need to remember their wives may have carried on a conversation with a four year old most of the day and they are ready for an adult conversation. Wives need to talk. They need it more than men.

Wives need to talk about their day. They need to share their triumphs and their troubles. They may not have any major event to tell you about but it's important they tell you anyway.

Husbands must give undivided attention to their wives each day. This conveys the message that their wives are important to them and they are worth time and attention.

This is huge for wives. They must feel they are their husband's top priority. This also keeps the lines of communication open.

Never go to bed with angry feelings unresolved. The Bible tells us that all become angry from time to time. But according to Ephesians 4:26 we must be very careful how we handle anger. The verse says: *Be ye angry, and sin not: let not the sun go down upon your wrath*.

Another way of saying this is (my paraphrase); *when you are angry, do not sin, but deal with your anger before you end your day*. Couples who talk each day can't help but put to bed problems before they put themselves to bed each night.

A fourth way husbands can help their wives feel secure is by never giving their wives reasons to become jealous. Husbands should be careful when interacting with other women. They should be perceptive and cautious of situations which might cause their wives to feel anxiety or uneasy.

Husbands should never be alone with other women. They run the risk of possibly being accused of an indiscretion. Even if nothing occurs, the mere appearance can cause unnecessary feelings and wives may feel threatened.

Husbands should be careful in complimenting other women. I make a practice of never complimenting another lady's looks or clothes. Does that mean I do not notice them? You are missing the point. There are two very important reasons why I've chosen to do this.

First and most important, most wives feel their own personal looks are declining. Even though she is the most gorgeous woman in the world to her husband, she needs to hear from her husband that she is the most gorgeous woman in the world.

When men compliment other women in the presence of their wives, their wives many times feel insecure. The compliment towards other women reinforces that insecurity. The compliments by husbands on looks and clothes should stay with their wives.

Secondly, husbands may send wrong signals to other women who they are complimenting. Those women may not be receiving compliments at home and when another man compliments them, they may read a signal of possible interest in them that was not intended. Husbands, save the compliments for your wives.

A fifth way husbands can help their wives feel secure is not comparing them to other women, especially the husband's mother. Your wife will never be your mom and aren't you glad? Your wife is unique and special.

She will never cook just like your mom. She will never keep house just like your mom. She will never wait on you hand and foot like your mom. Comparison to your mom will only tear your wife down and make her feel like you think she doesn't measure up to what you expected.

Husbands should complement their wives from one to three times daily. Thank her for doing the laundry. Thank her for fixing the evening meal. Thank her for dropping that bill off at the post office.

Tell her she really looks nice today. Tell her that dress really looks nice on her. Treat her like a queen and you might be surprised how she treats you.

Homemaker

The second basic need of women is to be homemakers. This need is interwoven with the desire to have children and provide a good environment for them to grow up in.

Wives are born with a **need to build their nests**. Wives transform a cold plain house into a warm inviting home. How do they do it? They match the curtains with the carpet and make sure there's toilet paper and soap in the bathrooms. They add what-knots, do-dads, knick-knacks, dust catchers, etc.

Wives have E.W.P. (*Extra Wife Perception*). They *just know* when the furniture needs re-arranging or replacing, the carpets need cleaning, and the walls need a fresh coat of paint.

Wise husbands will recognize this need and encourage their wives by empowering them to continually *feather their nests* making the house a home.

Wives want a *safe place* for their children. Wise husbands will do all they can to provide that place. It's the husband's responsibility to make sure the house is kept in good working order, the plumbing works, the washing machine washes and the doors close, do not squeak, and are secure.

The real economic world that most families find themselves in requires two paychecks to provide the financial needs of the family. This is not the time or place to argue if, or women should work outside the home. The fact is statistics show that over 77% of married women with children between ages 6 and 17 *are employed outside the home.*

Another statistic that most women would heartily agree with is that almost 100% of those women who work outside the home have a second fulltime job waiting for them when they return back home from work.

Grocery lists have to be made. Meals must be planned and prepared. Clothes must be purchased, washed, pressed and put away.

School registrations must be completed. Schoolbooks and supplies must be purchased. Homework tutoring must be completed before bedtime. Most of these tasks and a multitude of others fall to the woman of the house.

If the wife works outside the home, the husband should help with chores around the house. Husbands should look for ways to relieve wives of the stress of trying to *get it all done* alone. Men should say things like; *children, lets clear the table for your mom and Sally you wash, Billy you dry.*

Men should be alert when the laundry is backing up and *put a load or two of clothes in the washer*. They should also note *when the dryer stops, grab a basket, fold the clothes and have them ready for the wife to put away.*

Cleaning the house should be a family activity. Each family should participate. The husband should do the heavy jobs like vacuuming. The children should have assigned tasks.

Now back to our story…….

One day, three men were hiking and unexpectedly came upon a large, raging, violent river. They needed to get to the other side, but had no an idea how to do so.

The first man prayed to God, saying, "Please God, give me the strength to cross this river."

POOF! God gave him big arms and strong legs, and he was able to swim across the river in about two hours, after almost drowning a couple of times.

Seeing this, the second man prayed to God, saying, "Please God, give me the strength and the tools to cross this river.

POOF! God gave him a rowboat and he was able to row across the river in about an hour, almost capsizing the boat a couple of times.

The third man saw how this worked out for the other two, so he also prayed to God saying, "Please God, give me the strength and the tools...and the intelligence...to cross this river."

POOF! God turned him into a woman. She pulled out a map, hiked upstream a couple hundred yards, and walked across the bridge that was just around the bend all the time.

ACTION STEPS

1. What are some basic needs of most wives?

_____

_____

_____

_____

2. What are some things I can do to meet the needs of my wife?

_____

_____

_____

_____

3. What important thing(s) did I learn from

this chapter?

_____

_____

_____

_____

Chapter 4

King of His Castle

The preacher spent his whole sermon relating the evils of sin and how all men are sinners with no exceptions.

At the end of the sermon he asked a rhetorical question; *does anyone here think he is perfect and without sin*? He had only to wait a few seconds before a man near the back of the auditorium rose slowly to his feet.

Roy enjoys deer hunting. He harvested this nice 340lb, 8-point buck.

The pastor asked the man who had the audacity to stand after such a fiery sermon:

"Sir, do you really think you are perfect and completely without sin?"

You'll never believe how the man responded and why, but we will find out at the end of this chapter.

Some women marry their husbands and then set out to change them into what they want them to be.

Wives sometimes make the mistake of believing that their husbands think the way they do. Just as men and women are different physically and emotionally, they are also different in the way they think.

He may spit in the sink. Leave his shoes by his chair every night. He may miss the hamper more times than he hits it with his dirty clothes. Complaining or nagging won't change him.

Wives should work hard to appreciate the good qualities of their husbands. Be thankful he doesn't chew tobacco and spit in the sink. Thank the Lord for husbands who work hard to provide for their families.

Husbands who love and are faithful to their wives and their wives alone should be cherished and appreciated. Wives can turn those chores like picking up his shoes and clothes into a labor of love.

Just as women have at least two basic needs, so do men. Perceptive wives will concentrate on discovering their husband's needs and do their best to meet them.

What are the two basic needs of men?

1. *EGO*

A man's first basic need involves his ego. This need finds its history with the way God created him. God created men to protect, provide for, and be pathfinders for their families. Just as women make houses homes,

Common Sense FAMILIES

men provide the foundational strength upon which the home is built.

Men are built with the emotional need to be defenders of their families. They must feel that their families know they can count on them to keep them safe.

Men feel a deep responsibility to provide the needs of their families. God placed within their DNA the strong desire to provide protection, food, shelter, and clothing for their families.

God also created men to provide leadership. Men feel the need to select, take charge, and lead their families down safe pathways in life.

How can wives appreciate and meet their husband's need to be the leader in the home? There are a number of things she can do.

Wives should learn to *appreciate the uniqueness* of their husbands. Constantly focusing on shortcomings and weaknesses will cause wives to overlook the strengths and value their husbands bring to them and their marriage.

Wise women will *never tear their husbands down*. Belittling, taking them down a notch, reminding them that they are short, fat, do not make as much money as others, etc. will deflate their egos. They will feel inadequate and failures in their wives' eyes because they do not measure up to wives' expectations.

How husbands and wives communicate in public is very important. Wise women will not criticize their husbands in front of others.

Women who criticize or talk down to their husbands in front of others demoralize them. They feel that they have lost respect in the eyes of those who heard the criticism.

Wise women will build their husbands up in front of the children. Children begin early forming opinions about their parents. Mothers should help their children learn to respect their fathers and his role in the home. They should also be taught to appreciate all that he does for the family.

How can wives do this? By bragging on their husbands in front of the children. Telling the children in their father's presence; children, you have the best dad.

He works so hard so we can have a good place to live. He makes sure we have plenty of food to eat. Your dad is a good man. Many children grow up without good fathers.

Husbands need building up in private by their wives. Wise women should understand that one of the main goals in their husband's lives is to feel that they are meeting the needs of their wives.

Not just the material needs, but also the physical and emotional needs of their wives. Wives should tell their husbands they're proud of them. Husbands need to feel that they are successful in their wives' eyes.

2. *Physical Need*

Man's second basic need is physical and has two parts.

FOOD

I'm sure you've heard the old expression that the way to a man's heart is through his stomach. There is a lot of truth to that statement. Men need food!

Many wives work outside the home in our modern culture. Men's attitudes and emotions are affected by food or the lack thereof.

Providing a wholesome hot nourishing meal each day may do more to impact a marriage in a positive way than many couples realize. By providing a hot meal for your husband, he is being told: *I care about what you need*.

Wise wives will not mention or discuss nonemergency problems before their husbands finish supper. This is difficult for many women.

Women want to express their feelings much more quickly than men. Husbands are just arriving home. They may have been confronted throughout the day with the complaints and problems of others.

They're looking for the solace of being the king of their castles. They're hungry, tired and sometimes grouchy. Wives might be amazed at the transformation they see in their husbands within an hour or two if eating a hot meal with an adoring family.

SEX

Sex is another basic need of husbands.

Generally, men's sexual drive, desire and needs are much stronger than women's.

Hebrews 13:4a reminds us that *Marriage is honorable in all, and the bed undefiled.* God invented sex and it is pure, valuable, and designed to meet the needs of both mates.

There is nothing dirty or sinful about the sexual relationship between husbands and wives. Married couples should not feel bad or guilty.

They should not make their spouses feel they are not interested in having sex and they're only doing it to satisfy their mate's needs.

Wives should keep in mind, the same thing is true for husbands as well, that their bodies are not their own. When a man and woman get married, they become one flesh. Each of their bodies belongs to the other.

Unfortunately, wives sometimes withhold themselves from their husbands to punish them or to get their ways. This is a dangerous thing to do. Couples who isolate themselves in this intimate area of marriage usually have deep-seated marital problems.

If the sexual relationship in marriage is used as a weapon, it may be the one thing that becomes the beginning of the end of the marriage. The need for sexual satisfaction is built deep within men.

Wives who minimize this and fail to understand or appreciate its importance to their men are planting seeds that may grow destructive fruit in the marriage.

Husbands should remember to be gentle with their wives. Men are stronger than their wives and must be careful not to make the experience a painful one for their wives.

Husbands should learn what pleases their wives and what harms the experience for them. They should make the experience as beneficial for their wives as they want for themselves.

If married partners continue to have difficulties in this area, it might be wise to seek an experienced Christian counselor who might be able to help.

Husbands and wives should be careful about sharing intimate information about sexual problems with friends and family. Those people may not be qualified to offer advice and could do more harm than good. It is not wise for too many people to know about a couple's private problems.

Husbands and wives should *never go to bed angry* at one another. The Bible makes this clear in Ephesians 4:24 *instructing us not to allow the sun to go down on our anger.* We're being told that we are to settle our differences before we go to bed.

Wives should tell their husbands they are good lovers. The intimate sexual relationship between husbands and wives plays a vital role in men's egos. Men need to feel that they are pleasing their wives in this private part of their relationship.

Wow Honey, you are something else. Statements like that reassure men that their wives are pleased with them and that they are measuring up in their wives' eyes.

Wow you're such a good lover. Husbands need to know that they are meeting the sexual needs of their wives. If they believe the wife is pleased with their sexual performance, they do not have to prove anything to the world.

Nothing will make a man feel more like a man than knowing he is pleasing his wife. *If a man is given steak at home, he will not settle for bologna on the road.* Enough said!

Back to our story.......

The preacher spent his whole sermon relating the evils of sin and how all men are sinners with no exceptions.

At the end of the sermon he asked a rhetorical question; *does anyone here think he is perfect and without sin*? He had only to wait a few seconds before a man near the back of the auditorium rose slowly to his feet.

The pastor asked the man who had the audacity to stand after such a fiery sermon: "Sir, do you really think you are perfect and completely without sin?"

The man quickly answered, "No sir, I'm not standing up for myself, but for my wife's first husband."

ACTION STEPS

1. What are some basic needs of my husband?

_____

_____

_____

_____

2. What can I do to improve in meeting my husband's needs?

_____

_____

_____

_____

_____

3. What important thing(s) did I learn

from this chapter?

_____

_____

_____

_____

_____

_____

Chapter 5

We Need to Talk

There was a man who lived in upstate New York and was tired of the cold weather, so he decided to spend a few days in Florida. His wife was on a business trip at the time in another state. He called to let her know what he was doing and instructed her not to return to New York, but meet him in Florida.

When he arrived in Florida, he sent an e-mail to let her know he had arrived safely. But he accidentally trans-posed two letters in the e-mail address. Instead of ending up in his wife's inbox, the e-mail went to a little old lady in Iowa. Her pastor husband had died the day before.

The little old lady opened her computer and checked her e-mail.

She read the e-mail, screamed, fainted on the spot, and fell out of her chair.

Her family and friends rushed in to see what had happened and found her lying on the floor. When they read the e-mail they understood why she fainted.

We'll discover what made her faint at the end of the chapter.

Husbands and wives must learn to communicate effectively if they are to understand and meet the needs of each other.

There are a number of principles of communication, which are important for married couples. Ephesians 4:25-30 describes these wonderful principles.

Principle 1 - *Married couples should be honest and truthful with each other at all times.* Paul told the Ephesians *to put away lies and dishonesty and tell the truth.*

Marriage partners must be able to trust each other. *Trust* is the most important quality in marriage. Without trust between husbands and wives, it will be impossible to develop and maintain a close relationship.

Principle 2 - *Married couples should be willing to discuss any subject that is important to their mates*. Things that irritate or bother one mate should be openly discussed with the other. Little things can become big problems if left to harbor and fester in the marriage.

Little things must be brought out in the open and talked about. Failure to address the little things will cause them to be replayed over and over in one's mind and may result in resentment, animosity, and pronouncement of guilt on the mate.

Couples should never tell their mates what they are saying is dumb or stupid. Those two words should be barred from the household conversation altogether.

Principle 3 - *Anger, hurt feelings, disappointments, etc. should be shared in an appropriate way with mates.* It's much better to talk about it than let it fester for days and create bigger problems between husbands and wives.

Husbands and wives should be willing to listen to the other express their needs and feelings. They should be careful not to interrupt or tell the other mate they shouldn't feel that way.

Principle 4 - *Married couples should work at developing interest in their spouse's interests and opinions.* Husbands and wives should seek to make mates feel important.

They should let them know their ideas are valuable, and they want to hear what they have to say. Mates should be careful not to jump on, interrupt, or say things to spouses simply because they're expressing their wants and desires.

Spouses should become interested in the things that are important to their mates. How can husbands and wives develop interest in things that are important to their mates?

One great way is to ask questions about things they are interested in. The key is expressing, exhibiting, and actively showing real interest in their mates and what interests them.

Principle 5 - *Married couples should keep their emotions under control.* The Scriptures teach us in Ephesians 4:26 that *we will become angry from time to time but the important thing is not to allow anger to become sinful.* It is possible to become angry and not allow that anger to consume us to the point of ruling us.

Anger and uncontrolled emotions can cause a breakdown in communication within the home. When we become angry, we may say too much or not say anything at all. Neither one of these extremes is good and can drive a deep wedge between husbands and wives and hinder their ability to talk to each other.

Moms and dads should keep in mind the way they react and the techniques they use in dealing with anger may leave an image forged in the minds of their children that may be repeated by their children later in life when dealing with their own children.

How well do you handle anger? Your mate says or does something that upsets you, how should you respond? Be very careful about speaking before you've had time to think about what you're going to say.

Words said in anger may be forgiven, but may never be forgotten. Words that hurt could eventually cause the marriage to fall apart.

The author's first funeral in his first pastorate was a young child who drown in a backyard swimming pool. The drowning was an accident and just one of those unfortunate things that happen in life.

The mother felt severe guilt, which led to deep periods of depression. In the heat of an argument her husband yelled, "You killed my baby." He didn't mean to harm his wife, but the words crushed her emotionally.

The husband apologized but the damage was done. She never forgot what he had said and she never got past it. They are divorced today.

The real issue was grief. They were both hurting. Instead of grieving together they grew apart. The eruption was a symptom but not the cause.

How should one deal with anger? He should identify why he is angry. What he is angry at? Sometimes the issue is very small and not the real problem.

The issue becomes the catalyst that leads to an eruption culminating in harsh words between mates. One should look at the reason for his anger rather than allowing the emotion of anger to get out of control.

One must find the cause and not just the symptom. Overreacting usually is a result of overreaching when one becomes angry.

Principle 6 - *Couples should remember timing is important when discussing issues or dealing with problems*. Fatigue and hunger can contribute to inflammatory words, heated exchanges, and anger that escalate out of control.

Mates will be more irritable and less levelheaded when they become angry. Mates should be slow to speak when they are angry at each other. They should wait until the heat of the moment passes so things can be discussed on a more peaceful plain.

Principle 7 - *Couples should remember technique is important*. One should try his best not to overreact. Husbands and wives interacting in conversation over an issue or problem must be careful not to allow it to escalate into a much bigger problem.

The temptation is to *get one up* on the mate. He said that about me, so I'm going to say this about him. Before you know it, a laundry list of complaints about each other is hung out in the open for all to see.

There are no *winners or losers* when couples get angry and argue with one another. **Husbands and wives should never scream, yell, or raise their voices at each other.**

Mates should commit to themselves and to the Lord that they are not going to raise their voices in anger at their mates.

Wives should be careful about using tears to get their way. Tears may work on mates for a little while. At some point husbands will no longer communicate personal issues or problems to their wives.

Husbands and wives should sit down together and discuss the problem at hand. Sometimes couples try to talk to each other at a distance.

Sometimes they try to do this in separate rooms or at the other end of the house. The kitchen table is a great place to discuss issues.

Facing each other, seeing each other's countenance and facial expressions and the emotions during the conversation will help mates better understand the feelings of the other.

Stick to the subject. Do not allow other offenses or issues to be brought into the discussion at that point. They can be discussed at another time. *Stick to the issue at hand.*

Principle 8 - *Couples should share tasks and responsibilities in the home.*

> Ephesians 4:28 talks about stealing; *Let him who stole steal no more, but rather let him labor, working with his hands the thing which is good, so that he may have something to give to him who needs.* The biblical marital application is; *do not steal your husband' or wife's time.*

Many wives work outside the home in today's society. Men tend to think that housework, laundry, preparing meals, helping kids with homework, etc. are things that the wives should do. Men tend to be lazy when it comes to working around the house.

A poll a few years ago indicated the average wife and mother spends approximately *27 to 30 hours per week* performing home-related tasks. The same poll indicated that men spend approximately *1½ hours per week* helping around the house.

Husbands who want wives to help with the financial needs by working outside the home have an obligation and responsibility to help their wives in the home.

Husbands should help their wives without being asked. They should be alert, looking for ways to help their wives around the house and with the children.

Men, who are inconsiderate, lazy, and unwilling to help their wives around the house and with the children, communicate a lack of appreciation for what their wives do. This may cause wives to become resentful and angry.

Wives work full-time jobs outside the home only to return home to full-time jobs as well. Husbands, who plop down in their recliners, grab their TV remotes and do nothing to help their wives while they are cooking, cleaning, and taking care the children, are taking advantage of and mistreating their wives. This simply is not right.

How can husbands help their wives? Take on the responsibility for setting the table for the evening meal. This will teach the children by example, how they should help their mates later on in life.

Fill glasses with ice and pour the drinks for supper. Little things send a big message that husbands understand and appreciate how hard wives work.

Husbands should help their wives make the bed in the morning. Two people making a bed together takes very little time and it takes about a third of time than if one person makes the bed alone.

Men, ask your wives to purchase a shower scrub brush and hang it in the shower. Once a week, before you get out of the shower, take the brush and scrub down the shower for your wives. Tell your wives that you will be responsible for cleaning the bathroom commodes also.

Throw a load or two of laundry in the washer and dryer now and then. Children produce a great deal of dirty clothes and staying ahead of the laundry often is very difficult for wives. This will help them and also ensure there will be clean clothes when the family needs them.

Principle 9 - *Married couples should always seek to build up their mates and not tear them down.* This principle is found in Ephesians. What one says, how he says it, and the gestures used when he says it will define communication that edifies and builds up or communication, which corrupts and tears down.

An example would be, *honey you are a flathead,* is corrupt communication and tears down. *Honey, you are so levelheaded* edifies and builds up your mate. *Honey, you are so stingy* versus you're *so thrifty, and you really stretch our money. Honey, your face would stop a clock* versus *honey, when I look at you, time stands still*.

We should recite in our minds what we are thinking about saying before we open our mouths and say a word to our mates. We should consider how it might be received.

Smiling, nodding shows our mates they have our undivided attention and they are important to us and will make a difference in our communication. Mates need to feel that their spouses are supportive and interested in what they have to say.

Mates are not always looking for someone to solve their problems; they may just be looking for someone to listen.

Looking at your mate while they're talking to you is so important. Do not allow yourself to be distracted and indicate to your mate that they are not important to you.

Principle 10 - *Learn how to forgive but also how to say I'm sorry.* Whoever invented the expression *love is never having to say you're sorry*, knew nothing about what love is.

True love requires husbands and wives to learn to say I'm sorry. *Honey, I'm so sorry. I didn't mean to hurt your feelings.*

Love requires us to forgive. Genuine forgiveness appreciates and accepts our mate's apology for the hurt feelings or problems they have caused.

Husbands and wives who wish to communicate must learn to say I'm sorry and also how to forgive. It would be great if we were perfect, but we are not.

We are going to say things and do things that will cause hurt feelings in our mates. It will happen! The only way to remedy this is to ask for and grant forgiveness when asked.

A woman who'd been married 19 years kept a running list of her husband's offenses including the dates they occurred. She sought marital counseling for her and her husband.

The marriage counselor told the woman that a list like she had been doing was harboring hard feelings toward her husband. She must forgive her husband of all the things on the list. Then you should destroy the list.

I'll keep the list here for a few days if you'd like until you've had a chance to think and pray about this. The lady responded, I will ask for forgiveness. But please do not destroy that list. It's the only copy I have.

A good exercise for couples to do; face each other, take each other by the hand, look the other person in the eyes and do the following:

Husbands first say to your wives, please forgive me if I've hurt your feelings or done anything wrong to harm you. Now ladies, tell your husbands, I forgive you and I'm going to forget.

Wives say to your husbands, please forgive me if I've hurt your feelings or done anything wrong to harm you. Now husbands, tell your wives, I forgive you and I'm going to forget.

Now the same time, both of you say to each other, Honey, I love you.

Now let's return to our story.......

There was a man who lived in upstate New York and he was getting tired of the cold weather, so he decided to go to Florida. His wife was on a business trip at the time so he called her to let her know what he was doing and to ask her not to return to New York but to meet him in Florida.

When he arrived he sent her an e-mail to let her know he arrived safely, but transposed a few letters in the e-mail address. Instead of going to his wife, the e-mail went to a little old lady who was a pastor's wife in Iowa. Her husband had died the day before.

The little old lady turned on her computer to check her e-mail. She read the e-mail, screamed and fainted on the spot.

Her family and friends rushed in to see what was the matter and found her on the floor. When they read the e-mail they understood why she fainted...

Dearest darling just wanted you to know
I arrived safely.

I love and miss you.

Looking forward to you being with me
tomorrow.

Love, your husband SAM

PS, it sure is hot down here...

Good communication is absolutely
essential between husbands and wives.

Misunderstandings are inevitable from time
to time, but can be corrected and the situation
remedied by daily times reserved to talk with
one another.

ACTION STEPS

1.   How important is communication

between husbands and wives?

_____

_____

_____

_____

2.   What are some areas of communication

with my spouse that I need to work on?

_____

_____

_____

_____

3. What important lesson(s) did I learn from

this chapter?

_____

_____

_____

_____

Chapter 6

Things Have To Change

One bright and sunny Saturday

afternoon, two brothers-in-law were riding

down the road on the way to completing a small project. The older of the two was in his early 30s and the younger his late 20s.

The older man confided in the younger that he was concerned that his two sons ages 10 and 11 might follow in his footsteps and begin a habit that may cause an addiction which could last a lifetime. The young man smoked his first cigarette when he was a little boy and now 20 years later the habit had become an addiction. The addiction required almost hourly satisfaction.

The man knew his boys would probably follow his example and begin a lifelong habit that would impact them financially, hurt them physically, and follow them like a shadow for the rest of their lives.

So the two men together made a commitment to themselves and to the Lord that day that they would stop smoking immediately. They threw their cigarettes and cigarette lighters out the window of the old 1954 Chevy pickup truck hoping to never smoke again.

That older man was my father and the younger man my uncle. My father never smoked another cigarette because he made a life-changing commitment that day.

Changes usually are not easy. But changes can be made in our homes. Life-changing commitments can completely alter the destructive courses are homes are cascading down.

Change comes only when there is a willingness to change in the hearts of family members. Change may be necessary in order to develop the type of homes that God intended for us.

One can respond to God's command to change in a variety of ways. He can become angry because his shortcomings and faults are brought front and center in his life forcing him to face them. One can minimize or rationalize behavior and choose to ignore the obvious and refuse to change.

We should ask the question: *What changes do I need to make to be the person God wants me to be in order for my home to be all that it can be?*

Why should we be willing to change? There are at least three reasons.

The *first reason* we should change is because *God instructs us to change*. Ephesians 4:17 teaches us that as Christians we are no longer to continue living like the unsaved person lives; *This I say therefore, and testify in the Lord, that you should not walk from now on as other nations walk, in the vanity of their mind.*

One of the greatest things that hinder non-Christians from becoming Christians is the failure of Christians to make Christ-oriented changes in their lives.

The *second reason* we should change is because of *self-respect.* This is reinforced in verse 28; *Let him who stole steal no more, but rather let him labor, working with his hands the thing which is good, so that he may have something to give to him who needs.*

One can appreciate and love others if he respects himself. If one loves and is at peace with himself, then he will love, appreciate and be at peace with his family members.

A *third reason* why we should change is *because harmony in the home depends on it.* This is reinforced in Ephesians 5:21; *submitting yourselves to one another in the fear of God.*

The husband and wife become one when they are united in marriage. Although they are separate and unique individuals, they now are united in one identity. This is called the one flesh relationship in scripture. Each mate becomes part of the other.

It's much like a physical part of one's body. One is concerned for and takes care of the needs of his body. The same is true with that of one's mate. One must place the needs of the mate above his needs. This will require adjustments and changes in one's own life.

When should change take place? Ephesians 5:8 sheds light on this; *you were once darkness, but now you are light in the Lord; walk as children of light.* Many people would like things to change. But there is a 180-degree difference between having a desire and making a decision. Change takes place when one moves from desire to decision.

There are four steps, which must be taken if there is to be genuine change in the home:

Step 1: **There must be an ATTITUDE of WILLINGNESS to make changes.**

If one has become so entrenched in his or her own world with an unwillingness to compromise and make changes in his personal life, then change will never come to that person. The home will suffer because of it and God's plan will never be fully realized.

Step 2: **One must sincerely ATTEMPT to make changes.**

Mentioned earlier in the chapter, when this author was about eleven years old, he had the unique experience of watching his father quit smoking.

His father smoked one to two packs of cigarettes each day. There were a couple of things I learned by observing this major change in my father's life.

One important thing was that change required a major step and not halfway measures. My father didn't just reduce the number of cigarettes he smoked each day by a quarter, half or two-thirds.

He not only threw away all the remaining cigarettes he had purchased but he also threw away an expensive lighter that he used to ignite them.

My father understood correctly that this major change required a full and complete commitment on his part. He couldn't halfway quit because there is no such thing.

I also learned that change is hard. My father was a smoker for about twenty years. Smoking was a part of his identity.

It was not easy for him to stop smoking. But he did stop! He replaced his cigarettes with chewing gum. I watched him struggle and fight an inward battle with himself.

Each day he gained ground until one day he no longer wanted or needed a cigarette. The battle was hard, but the outcome was worth the struggle.

My father is now in his 80s and is 40+ years removed from that memorable day when he made the decision to quit smoking. I'm sure his life was extended by many years, and we all are blessed because he was willing to do the hard thing and make an important change in his life.

Change is usually not easy. But God-guided, family-impacting change can transform families into the place of peace and happiness God intended the home to be.

How do we develop an attitude of change? We must first put aside excuses for failing to change. Seeking refuge behind the wall of claiming inability to change is just an excuse.

That's just the way I am and I cannot change is no excuse for failing to attempt change. *I cannot change because of the way I was raised* is not a valid reason for failing to change.

We cannot blame others for failure to make needed changes in our lives. Parents, spouses, circumstances or other entities may have contributed to where we may be in life, but they should not be used as an excuse to keep us from where we need to go.

We live our own lives and are responsible for our actions. We cannot use the crutch of self-pity to excuse our lack of determination to make the hard changes. B*ehavior is learned,* and change requires us to *learn a better way*.

How do we develop an attitude of change? Secondly, remember that the past cannot be changed.

If we are to change our families, we must determine that we will forgive and forget. We must make a heartfelt decision to forgive. Genuine forgiveness will result in putting past hurts and disappointments *of our spouse's* behind us and never bring them up again.

Jesus shows us how to do this. He forgave our sins and promised they would forever be buried in the sea of God's forgetfulness, never to be mentioned again by anyone.

We must make a conscious decision to *forgive and forget, throw away our lists of our spouse's faults and shortcomings* and *never revisit or mention them again*.

How do we develop an attitude of change? Thirdly, we must realize that things can be different and the present can be changed.

The present is now; it's today! Today is changeable! We deal with life and make life changes in the present. The future pages of our families can be written differently if we make changes now.

Isaiah 1:18 reminds us that the Lord invites us to *come to Him NOW*. Now is always the time for change. When God's Word instructs, the Holy Spirit convicts and convinces, and our heart tells us to change, this is the time for change.

Step 3: The APPROACH to change is crucial.

> Ephesians 5: 15; *see then that you walk circumspectly, not as fools, but as wise*, reminds that we are to walk cautiously.

What does that mean? We must be perceptive to what is going on in the lives of our family members and observe how the world is impacting them.

What is a proper approach to making changes? First, a plan for change should be developed. Ephesians 4:21-23 provides insight for developing a plan for change:

> *If indeed you have heard Him and were taught by*

Him, as the truth is in Jesus. For you ought to put off the old man (according to your way of living before) who is corrupt according to the deceitful lusts, and be renewed in the spirit of your mind. God provides a plan for making changes to husbands and wives. The Word of God instructs us to hear Christ.

Hearing Christ begins with knowing Christ personally so He can speak to us. We are instructed to listen to what Christ has to say.

He encourages us to *come to Him with our heavy burdens and He will give us rest.* He wants to help us carry the family burdens. He wants our homes to be *places of rest.*

Homes will not be places of rest and function according to God's plan unless both husbands and wives know Christ as Lord and Savior. The biblical plan cannot be properly understood and implemented until both husband and wife are in a personal relationship with Christ.

Not only do husbands and wives need to hear the voice of Christ but also they must be receptive to the teachings of Christ. Just hearing the voice of Christ is not enough. We must be responsive to what He instructs us to do.

A lifestyle change is necessary. If change is to occur in our families, then specific changes must take place in our personal lives. When we hear the voice of Christ with specific instructions from the Holy Spirit, we must confess and commit to change the way we are living. We are to do away with the old way of doing things and form a new way of living.

Step 4: The ACCOMPLISHMENT through change will be tremendous.

What are some of those wonderful ACCOMPLISHMENTS that may be realized? Men will assume their proper roles in the family. The men will earn the respect of their wives and children. Men will look forward to and be happy in their own homes.

Women of the house will find their God-given roles and find fulfillment in their homes. Women will receive the attention, affection, and security they need and desire from their husbands.

They will earn the admiration and respect of their husbands and children. They will experience a sense of worth and value as moms and wives in their homes.

Children will grow up in homes where they understand future roles in their own families. Boys will learn by example the proper role of husbands and fathers.

Girls will grow up and become ladies. They will understand the biblical role of wife and mother. Boys and girls who later become young men and women will learn by example the kind of person to look for when choosing their own life mates.

Children will have a better chance of knowing Jesus Christ at an early age and how to mature and grow in the Christian life.

ACTION STEPS

1. Is willingness to make changes important to families? Why?

_____

_____

_____

_____

2. What is the most apparent change(s) we need to make in our home?

_____

_____

_____

_____

3. What is the greatest thing I gained

from this chapter?

_____

_____

_____

_____

Chapter 7

Teach Your Children Well

Claire, Lauren & Rachel three of Roy's five grandchildren.

Tony Campolo says his wife is a brilliant woman. She has a Ph.D. and is capable of pursuing a very profitable career. But she elected to stay home with her children when they were young.

Her decision didn't bother her at all except when other women would ask, *what do you do*? She would answer, *I'm a homemaker, and I stay home and take care of my children and my husband.* They would usually respond with *oh* and then ignore her from then on.

Mrs. Campolo came up with a response that has become a classic. At the end of the chapter we'll find out the response she now gives when asked what she does.

Ephesians 5:15 tells us that we are to - *understand what the will of the Lord is concerning how to grow children for God* (my paraphrase).

Children who become adults and live their lives for the Lord generally do this as a result of a process. It's not an overnight instantaneous transformation. Children must be taught, groomed, and exampled in how one should live for the Lord.

The older people become, the harder they are to reach for the Lord. Statistics bear this out. A large percentage of those who become Christians do so before the age of 15.

At each five-year interval, the percentage decreases. People who wait until middle age or near retirement age seldom come to know Christ.

Ages at which Americans say they accepted Christ and became a Christian

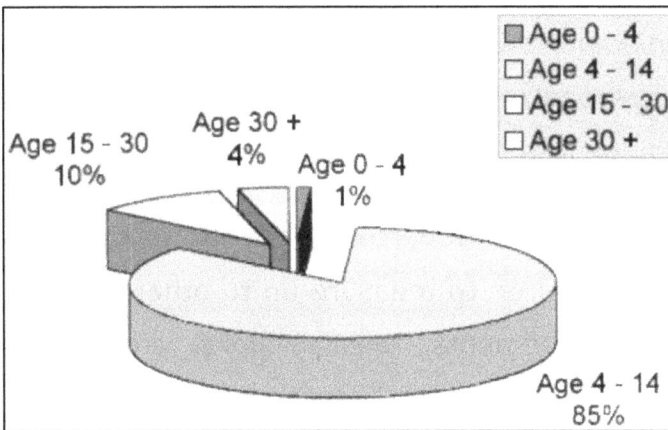

(The data in the pie graph comes from Nazarene Church Growth Research.)

The Scriptures teach us that as parents we have a responsibility to raise our children in the nurture and admonition of the Lord. There are three basic areas that we must understand and train our children in if they are to become adults for God, grow up, and become what God intended for them to be.

We should be reminded that how parents train their children, will directly *impact* their children and possibly their children's children.

The first area we will discuss is the *uniqueness of children.* Sometimes parents fail to recognize or appreciate the specialness and uniqueness of their children.

Parents tend to expect and even require their children to measure up to other children's accomplishments, talents, looks, etc. No two children are like.

Just as fingerprints reveal uniqueness of every human being, we should be reminded that God creates every child with a godly purpose and plan for his life, which is unlike anyone else's.

Children think as children. Sometimes parents expect their children to think, feel, and act like adults. Children do not have the experience or maturity to think like adults.

Parents think their children should think like they think. Children are incapable of that. Children think as children.

The apostle Paul teaches in one passage that when he was a child he thought as a child, but when he became an adult he acted like an adult. Paul understood the uniqueness and the differences between children and adults.

Parents should remember that each generation is different from the previous one. Children today are growing up in different schools, with different teachers, in a different world than their parents. Parents should remember their parents had a direct impact on the way they are raising their own children.

Parents sometimes make the mistake of expecting their children to grow up excelling in the same areas in which they excelled. Fathers and mothers may have been excellent athletes and they expect their sons and daughters to follow suit.

Their children may not be capable of doing what their parents did. They simply do not have the physical abilities or skills. Parents set impossible standards, which their children will never achieve.

Parents set academic standards, which are impossible for their children to attain. Parents may have earned straight A's and excelled in certain courses, but their children do not have the same ability.

Their children's strengths may not be in the field of academics. They do okay, but they will never rise to the level of their parents' achievements.

Parents' failure to achieve their personal hopes and dreams sometimes causes them to attempt to live out those hopes and dreams through the lives of their children. They literally force their children into areas, which the children are not interested in or capable of being successful, in order to achieve a sense of accomplishment in the parents' lives.

The family's name sometimes brings with it expectations of achievement and success that is simply not going to happen. Some children grow into adulthood and struggle the rest of their lives trying to measure up to the fact that they carry the name of famous, well accomplished parents.

The key is appreciating and accepting children for whom they are. Parents have been given the greatest gift apart from salvation, the children God has placed in their homes. With this great gift should come great appreciation and thankfulness for the children that God has chosen to enrich their lives with.

Parents should be reminded that the children God has placed in their homes are a vital part of God's kingdom plan. They were created to do kingdom work.

Parents have an awesome responsibility to raise these children in an environment that will prepare them to learn, live, and do the will of God.

Parents should double-check themselves to make sure they are not evaluating their children based upon the world's success standards. The world sets standards that are impossible for every child to reach.

The world showcases the most beautiful, most talented, most successful, best athletes, etc. while 99% of children will grow up never achieving standards of success set by the world. Parents should be careful not to fall or drag their children into that trap.

The *first standard* recognized by the culture is *beauty*. Children are judged in the cradle before they leave the hospital.

Some say the baby is cute. Others might say the baby is a little homely. Judgment is made solely on physical attributes. The beauty judgment continues throughout all ages and people tend to judge others based upon physical attributes.

A *second standard* in which the culture places great stock is *intelligence*. The better the grades the more recognition that's given.

Athletic ability is a *third standard* the culture places great emphasis on.

Material wealth is a *fourth standard* the culture uses as a measurement of success.

A true story is told of a minister who recently accepted the pastorate of a large church in a big city. The long awaited day came for his inaugural sermon as the new pastor.

A strange thing happened that Sunday morning. A few minutes before morning worship service was to begin, a downtrodden, weather beaten, poorly dressed, and unshaven man entered the lobby of the church.

It was obvious the folks around him were ignoring him, avoiding eye contact and moving away from him. They acted like he was not even there.

He made his way through the sanctuary doors and slowly walked down to the front row. No one greeted him, and it was obvious no one wanted to sit close to him. The apparently homeless man could sense many eyes on him and it was obvious he was not welcome in this congregation.

Service began with wonderful praise and worship choruses about the love of Jesus and how he cares for every soul. It was as though the hymns and choruses had been carefully selected to relay a message of God's love, especially for people like this homeless man.

The service moved along with prayer, the offering, and finally introduction of the new pastor. When the new pastor was introduced, the apparently homeless man rose to his feet. He began to make his way towards the steps to the stage.

The congregation was horrified! Ushers began to move toward this unkempt man hoping to stop him before he could get to the stage. It was too late. Before they could stop him, he mounted the stage.

The man pulled off his nasty ball cap and then his black wig, revealing the true identity of this man. He was not who he appeared to be.

The homeless man was not homeless at all. The man was the congregation's new pastor.

The message was very short that morning because it had already been preached when the homeless man mounted the stage and revealed his true identity. The congregation's heart was broken when they realized how they had judged this man not worthy of even a simple hello.

The great lesson here is obvious. We must not use the world's standards to judge our own children's success or worth. Lasting scars of inferiority may be left; not measuring up and feeling their parents are not pleased with them.

God *uses a different standard* to measure value and success.

The *first thing* God looks at is *character.* He looks at what is in the heart and that is how He measures true beauty. God made the rainbow, set the stars in the heavens, rolls the tides in and out and at his bidding, makes the sky blue, the snow white, and the fields green. Man's physical attributes are not what impress God.

The *second thing* God looks at is *spirituality*. God is looking for people who want to know, learn about, and serve him.

A *third thing* God looks at is people who have the right *attitude*.

The *fourth thing* God is looking for is people who will *live according to the instructions* found written in His Word.

Children are unique. They are not to be judged by the world's standards. They should be judged according to God's standards. Parents should accept and appreciate their children's uniqueness. There is not another one like that child in the entire universe.

A child's thought processes are different from an adult's thought processes. Things that are important to parents may not be important to children. A clean house, a low score on a round of golf, etc., generally mean little to children.

Things that are important to children should become important to parents. The simple things many times are the important things to children.

While playing in the yard or the park, the child may find a bird's nest fallen from a tree. This fascinates them.

They may come running with joy and excitement to show this great discovery to a parent. If a parent scolds or belittles the child indicating that this is not important to the parent, this may leave a lasting negative memory for the child.

Children are fascinated with video games in today's culture. Parents would be wise to become familiar with the games their children are playing.

When a child comes to a parent announcing a level of success in a videogame, parents should be complimentary, give a pat on the back and brag on the child for doing a good job. Parents should show interest in what their children are interested in and what is important to them.

A paper from school with a gold star for a good job should be received with joy and excitement for the achievement of their sons or daughters. When the child comes home and tells the parents I was called on to read in class today. The teacher told me I did a really good job. Parents should embrace this with both arms and reinforce the compliment given by the teacher. This was important to the child that particular day and it should be important to the parents also.

2. A *second area* that is important in training children for life is *building character with proper training*. Teach children to love others.

One way to teach children to love others is by showing love for widows. Check on widows from time to time and take the children along.

Look for opportunities to make life a little easier for the widows. Cut the grass. Deliver fresh vegetables from the garden. Drop a card anonymously in the mail with a $20 bill in it.

3. *The third area* that is important in training children for life is teaching them that the *comforts* and *necessities of life are rewards of hard work*.

Parents who are constantly giving to their children and never require sacrifice or work from their children are teaching the wrong lessons.

I secured a job at a fast food restaurant just after my 16th birthday. I saved my money for about six months hoping to purchase my own car by the time I received his license.

I saved about half the amount I would need to purchase a car. My father observed my hard work, thrifty spending, and clocklike saving.

My father loaned me the other half needed to complete the purchase of the automobile. I agreed to pay my father back with weekly installments from my paycheck until the debt was paid.

I repaid the debt and the car was mine free and clear. I learned a lesson about working hard and receiving reward from my labor.

This great lesson benefited me throughout my entire adult life. I sought to instill this same principle into the lives of my children.

Parents, who give their children everything never making them work for things they receive, are teaching them to expect something for nothing when they grow up.

They grow up and become adults living in a world expecting to receive everything their parents have and expecting to have it now. This may result in wrecked marriages and ruined lives.

I remember one couple that soon after they were married, moved into a new house. They borrowed heavily to purchase a new car for the young lady and a new pickup truck for the young man.

They accumulated thousands of dollars in credit card debt. They began to argue over money and it wasn't long until their storybook marriage ended in bankruptcy and divorce.

Children should be encouraged to take small part-time jobs when they become old enough. Dads should encourage their sons to earn extra money by cutting a few lawns, raking leaves in the fall, and to become creative in looking for opportunities.

Moms should encourage their daughters to take on babysitting jobs, help clean a neighbor's house, and other opportunities to earn some extra money.

Children who work will learn the value of hard work, the rewards of hard work, and the response by others to their hard work.

4. The fourth area that is important for training children for life is teaching them *adversity builds character*. Parents should not always try to protect their children and rescue them from disappointments and hardships in life.

I remember when I was eleven years old I learned about the Soap Box Derby that was held in our town every year. I approached my dad about helping me design and built a Soap Box Derby car.

My farther said he would help me design the car, find the materials and put it together. But I would first have to secure the sponsor to pay for it. I thought about who might be a good choice. I remembered a local businessman who attended our church and was a family friend. I mentioned this man to my father and he arranged for me to talk with the businessman.

I was excited! I had an idea of the car I would like to build. I rehearsed over and over in my mind the words I would say to this man. The day came and I just knew he would provide the money to build my new racing machine.

I told him of my desire to build my own car and enter the Soap Box Derby. It was hard, but I got the words out and asked him if he would consider sponsoring me in the Derby?

Mr. Bilbrey told me that he would love to help me but things were a little "tight" financially in his business right now. He was sorry but he couldn't sponsor me.

I was so disappointed. It seemed as though my young world was crumbling around me. But the sun came up the next day and life went on.

My father didn't rush in and rescue me from my disappointment by funding the racer. I learned something that day about money. I determined that I wanted to find a way to earn money. Soon after I secured a job as a paperboy delivering *The Bulletin*, the evening newspaper in our neighborhood.

Disappointments, discouragement, and adversity are part of life. Children learn how to handle big problems in life through lessons learned by handling small problems as children.

Parents fail when they do not allow their children to make mistakes and handle their small problems. Parents set their children up for failure later on in life because mistakes and big problems will surely come. If children have not developed methods of identifying, coping, and dealing with their problems as children, they will be lost in the adult world.

5. Children should be trained to develop positive outlooks and good attitudes. Parents

who want their children to have good outlooks and positive attitudes must example these in front of their children.

Parents, who see the negative in everything and grumble about everyone and everything, can expect their children to imitate the behavior they have been taught by their parents.

The first step in teaching children to have positive attitudes is displaying positive attitudes by the parents. There may be good reasons to complain, but parents should work hard at showing their children that complaining will only hurt the complainer.

Children watch closely how parents react to life situations. If parents are thankful there is a good chance their children will become thankful also.

Now Back to Mrs. Campolo's New Response.......

Tony Campolo says that his wife is a brilliant woman. She has a Ph.D. and is capable of pursuing a very profitable career. But she elected to stay home with her children when they were young.

Her decision didn't bother her at all except when other women would ask, *what do you do*? She would answer *I'm a homemaker. I stay home and take care of my children and my husband*. They would usually respond with *Oh* and then ignore her from then on.

Mrs. Campolo came up with this response when she was asked what she did: *I'm socializing two Homo sapiens in Judeo-Christian values so they'll appropriate the eschatological values of utopia. What do you do*?

They would often blurt out *I'm a doctor* or *I'm a lawyer* and wander off with dazed looks in their eyes.

ACTION STEPS

1. What is the most important thing to remember about children?

_____

_____

_____

_____

2. What are some areas I need to work on with my children?

_____

_____

_____

_____

3. What is the most valuable thing I

learned from this chapter?

_____

_____

_____

_____

_____

Chapter 8

The Hardest Part of Parenting

1961 Chevy Impala

The teenage boy worked almost 6 months in a fast food restaurant. He was approaching 16½ years of age. He saved his money in hopes of purchasing his own car.

He'd accumulated about half what was needed for the purchase of a 1961 Chevrolet Impala. Two tone colors of sky blue and white complete with chrome rims, a car that any boy his age would be proud to own.

His father loaned him the other half needed to purchase the car with the agreement that a portion of each paycheck would go towards repaying the debt. The young man was able to purchase the car but could only drive it with a licensed driver present.

He would have to wait a few more weeks, and then he would be old enough to take his driving test and earn his driver's license. The young man's father instructed him not to drive the car by himself until the learner's permit was replaced with his driver's license.

The young man stepped off the school bus one afternoon and couldn't resist just sitting in his new car and listening to the engine run. The family lived about 100 yards from the edge of the city limits.

He rationalized that it really wouldn't hurt to take the car for a short spin out in the country. After all, who would know?

Did he take the car for a spin in the country? At the end of the chapter we'll see what he did and what happened as a result.

Ephesians 6:1-4;
Children, obey your parents in the Lord, for this is right. Honor your father and mother, which is the first commandment with a promise, so that it may be well with you, and that you may live long on the earth. Fathers, do not provoke your children to wrath, but bring them up in the nurture and admonition of the Lord.

Children should be praised for good behavior and disciplined for bad behavior.

When should a child be disciplined?

Children should begin receiving discipline when they understand the word no. They are old enough at this point for discipline to begin. The Bible says that children are *to be raised in the nurture and admonition of the Lord.*

Fathers should remember that they are head disciplinarians and will give account before God for the way they raised their children.

There are four areas we will discuss about when children should be disciplined.

1. *When children move beyond established boundaries in the home, they should be corrected and disciplined.* These boundaries should be explained, well defined, and clearly understood by both parents and children. But when children cross those

boundaries, they must understand that there is a penalty they will have to pay.

Why is it important to establish boundaries in the home? Why is it important for children to understand that crossing boundaries will cost them something? Parents are preparing children to live in society.

Society has established certain boundaries that are not to be crossed. Society has established penalties that will be extracted from those who cross those boundaries. Parents, who do not teach their children at home how to live within boundaries, may one day see those children have problems in society.

Parents should teach their children how to live on their own in a world that will expect them to live by the rules. What are some boundaries that should be set in the home?

Not throwing a ball in the house, going through drawers, getting food from the refrigerator, opening closed doors without knocking and asking permission, playing in the fireplace, playing with siblings' things without permission, going outside without permission, crossing the street without permission, etc.

Parents should understand that it is their responsibility to discipline their children. If parents do not do it, no one else will.

Failure to set appropriate boundaries within the home will escalate into crossing greater boundaries in society later. Parents will harvest the whirlwind of misbehaving teenagers because they failed to plant seeds of discipline when the children were small.

2. Children should be disciplined when they directly *challenge parental authority*.

A parent instructs the child that the yard is to be mowed before the parent returns home from work in the evening. The son refuses to mow the grass in direct defiance of his father's instructions to mow the grass. That son must be disciplined.

A parent instructs the child to clean the den, dust the furniture, and vacuum the carpet. The work is to be completed before the parent returns in the evening from work. The parent returns home and finds the daughter has refused to do as she was instructed. The daughter should be punished.

The issue is not the grass or the den. The issue is the direct disobeying of parents' instructions and defying their authority. Parents should understand this is a huge problem.

By not confronting the disobedience and defiance of their authority, parents are planting seeds for bigger and more damaging problems later. Children who defy their parents when they are young will lie, disobey, verbally abuse, and sometimes even bring physical harm to their parents later on.

One cannot over emphasize how important it is to deal with this matter of direct challenges of parental authority. Parents must meet this head on and early on in the lives of their children.

Children should understand from an early age that parents say what they mean, and mean what they say. Children learn early when their parents do not follow through on what they say. They will come to the conclusion that they don't really mean it and therefore they don't have to abide by it.

But if children learn early that parents mean what they say and that there are consequences for failing to follow and do what their parents tell them, they will be better prepared to live in society and be successful in life.

Parents should remember their children's first impression of who God is, what God expects, and what God does, is learned from the example of their parents. If parents do not display this well before their children, children will not believe God's Word means what it says, will do what it says, or there is punishment for violating its' truths.

3. Children who *infringe upon the rights of others* should be punished.

Children who are not taught to respect the rights and properties of other children will most likely fail to respect the rights and properties of others later on in life when they are thrust out into society.

One example would be children playing with other children's toys. Abusing, damaging, or destroying toys of other children should not be tolerated. When children are visiting in someone else's home, they should be taught to respect the property and the privacy of the homes they visit. They should not be given free reign and should be challenged when they behave inappropriately in the homes of others.

Children should be taught to respect others in public settings. Church services, restaurants, and grocery stores are a few places where children should be taught how to behave and be disciplined for failing to behave properly.

Not littering, walking on the grass, and missing the trashcan in the restrooms, are examples of how children should be taught that other people have rights, and those rights should be respected.

4.   Children should be punished when they *violate God's laws of character* such as lying, cheating and stealing, to name a few. It may seem cute when a small child tells a little white lie. But it is a dangerous precedent to excuse and accept this behavior, even in young children.

Children who bring home other children's toys should be thoroughly questioned by parents. Stealing is wrong according to the Word of God. Whether it's a dime, a dollar, or a million dollars, stealing is stealing.

Children must learn early that stealing is wrong. Failure to discipline children who take little things provides an incubator that will hatch an adult who will steal big things.

Stealing may begin with something as small as a pencil, or a book from the library, but then may escalate to a bicycle, a car for an older teenager, and on you go.

Cursing and foul language is a direct violation of God's law. Children may seem cute when they use an off-color word because it's so out of character for their age, but please understand their off-color vocabulary will only increase, as they grow older. Parents, who don't want their children to use vulgar language shouldn't use vulgar language. Children repeat what they hear.

Cheating is violation of God's Word. Copying someone else's homework as a child may become the forerunner of cheating on the job as an adult. Cheating is one form of trying to take shortcuts in life. Children who cheat will be adults who will be looking for the easy way out in life.

How should children be punished?

Many in society today frown on the old tried-and-true punishment of spanking. It is not my place to say that spanking is for everyone. But the Bible has a great deal to say about corporal punishment.

Let's define proper and improper corporal punishment. There is a line that is not to be crossed when administering corporal punishment. Bruising, abusing, or causing bodily harm is improper and is also illegal.

One great benefit of spanking, it is over very quickly. The incident is dealt with, the violation is addressed, parents and children move on. Parents sometimes make more work for themselves with long drawn out forms of discipline that actually punish the parents as much, if not more than the children.

Ages of children require different forms of discipline. There is an age when spanking is not appropriate. This age should be based on the maturity of the child. When children reach pre-teen years, they are too old to spank. Spanking may create anger and rebellion.

Spanking should not be administered for small violations. Spanking should be reserved for larger offenses. Direct disobedience should be met head on and spanking is appropriate. The four major areas mentioned earlier are areas of discipline in which spanking is appropriate.

What should be used to spank a child? Great caution should be taken at this point. Electrical cords, ropes, belts and etc. easily leave marks and bruises and could result in injury to children and should not be used. A more appropriate approach is to use the open hand with younger children on their bottom or a light smack on their hand. A small paddle to the bottom, as they get a little older.

Children should never be slapped on the face or the head.

When children reach late elementary school, they are quickly becoming too old to spank. Spanking may force them to conform, but it may instill anger and rebellion because they're growing up and there are better ways to discipline them.

Restrictions of their cell phones, television viewing, visiting their friends, riding their bicycles, shopping at the mall and keeping their bedroom door open all the time are a few ways to consider.

How do you balance discipline and praise?

Praise and reward should be given to children for good behavior. Proverbs 25:11 reminds us how important encouraging words are to others: *A word fitly spoken is like apples of gold in pictures of silver. As a ring of gold, and an ornament of fine gold, so is a wise reprover upon a hearing ear.*

This principle rings true with our children as well. Kind words of encouragement and appreciation are a tremendous aid in helping our children develop the desire to behave properly.

Parents should remember 95% of the time their children's behavior is good. Parents sometimes sacrifice a good relationship they could have with their children because they dwell on the few times their kids misbehave. Parents should learn to punish, move forward and forget.

Constantly reminding children of their mistakes after they have been disciplined conveys to children that parents have not forgiven nor are they going to forget. It's a no-win scenario for the children, because they cannot please their parents.

This may create long-term spiritual ramifications as well. We convey to our children that God will not forgive nor will He forget and He will always be reminding them of the things they have done wrong.

Children should not be punished for normal accidents that happen. Children spill things from time to time. Children should not be spanked, hand slapped or screamed at for unavoidable accidents.

If a child intentionally throws his milk from his high chair to the floor, then that's a different matter. But children will be children and they will make mistakes.

Those kinds of mistakes should not be disciplined. Children should not be disciplined for being children.

Remember to praise children for good behavior. How can you do this? First of all, praise them with your words.

Proverbs 3:27 reminds us that we have a responsibility to give praise and not withhold it from those who deserve it: *Do not withhold good from those to whom it is due, when it is in the power of your hand to do it.*

When children complete tasks they have been assigned, parents should praise them for the good job they have done. Parents should be careful about nitpicking small imperfections in the task.

Children learn by example and experience. The more experience they gain, the better they will become at the task. Obviously, they will not be experts on their first attempt.

We should say "please" and "thank you" to our children. If we expect them to say "please" and "thank you" to others, they should know that we appreciate them and they learned that by how we speak to them.

When children are given tasks and complete them, we should always say thank you. *Thank you son for cutting the grass. Thank you Mary for cleaning the den today.* We are instilling in our children an attitude they will one day convey to their children.

Children should be praised for good behavior in public. *Johnny, Mommy was really proud of the way you sat so quietly in church. Thank you for being a good boy in church.*

Nodding your head in approval is a great encouragement to children. Physically patting your children on the back, and telling them what fine jobs they've done means a lot. A hug, smile, just touching them with your hand will go a long way.

Rewarding children with a special trip or going to a special place because of their great behavior encourages a child to want to please Mom and Dad.

Now back to our story.........

The teenage boy had been working almost 6 months in a fast food restaurant. He was approaching 16½ years of age. He saved his money in hopes of purchasing his own car.

He'd accumulated about half what was needed for the purchase of a 1961 Chevrolet Impala. Two tone colors of sky blue and white complete with chrome rims, a car that any boy his age would be proud to own.

His father loaned him the other half needed to purchase a car with the agreement that a portion of each paycheck would go towards paying back the debt. The young man was able to purchase the car but could only drive it with a licensed driver present.

He would have to wait a few weeks until he would be old enough to take his driving test and earn his driver's license. The young man's father instructed him not to drive the car by himself until the learner's permit was replaced with his driver's license.

The young man stepped off the school bus one afternoon and couldn't resist just sitting in his new car and listening to the engine run. The family lived about 100 yards from the edge of the city limits.

He rationalized that it really wouldn't hurt just to take the car for a spin out in the country. After all, who would know?

He placed the key in the ignition and started the car. The glass pipe mufflers sounded deep and mellow. The rumble of the motor shook the car with a subtle feeling of sheer power.

Before he could help himself, he mashed in the clutch, put the car in reverse, backed out of the driveway and headed out West 25th Street into the Madison County countryside.

He only traveled a few miles before returning back home. He drove the car back into the driveway as close to the original position as he could remember. He was hoping his father would not recognize the car had been moved.

He sat on the front porch when his parents pulled in the driveway arriving home from work. He noticed that his father glanced over at his car and then glanced at the young man on the porch.

He climbed the steps and stopped dead in his tracks. *Son, did you drive your car this afternoon*? The blood drained from the young man's face. How did his father know what he had done?

Yes sir, I just drove it around the block. There wasn't any traffic and I thought the car needed to be driven a little just to keep the battery charged.

Okay, he told his son. *Didn't I tell you not to drive the car without a licensed driver in the car with you*? *Hand me your keys* he said.

I'll still let you take your driving test next week. But you'll have to wait two weeks after you get your license before I'll give you the keys back and you can drive your car.

Well, that young man was me and that man was my dad. Those two weeks of walking past my newly purchased car knowing that I could be driving it if I hadn't blown it by disobeying my parents, taught me a valuable lesson about obedience.

My father chose just the right form of discipline to teach me the valuable teenage lesson I needed to learn.

**On the left: Albert Harris, Roy's father
with Roy on the right holding
granddaughter Lauren Harris.**

ACTION STEPS

1. What is the hardest part of being a parent?

_____

_____

_____

_____

2. In what ways do I need to make some improvements in the way I'm disciplining my child?_____

_____

_____

_____

_____

3. What was the most helpful thing I gained from this chapter?

_____

_____

_____

_____

_____

Chapter 9

Stranger in Our House

Marissa's 16th birthday presents from Pawpaw & Mimi. Pawpaw (this Author) built the Hope Chest and Mimi filled it with goodies.

Proverbs 20:11 -
Even a child is known by his own doings, whether his work is pure and whether it is right.

The young man passed his 12th birthday and was quickly on his way to becoming a teenager. The school system required young men to take home economics in the seventh grade and young women to take basic shop in the eighth grade.

One of the requirements of the home economics class was to learn basic things about cooking. One day he and others were required to prepare some snacks for the entire class. The young man's assignment was to bake oatmeal cookies.

The recipe for the cookies was written on a 3 x 5 card with a cartridge ink pen. Someone had spilled water on the card earlier causing the ink to run and some of the details of the recipe to become blurred.

The cookie batter was completed. The cookies were cut, shaped, and placed into the preheated oven. They smelled delicious when baking and were tempting while cooling on the counter.

The time came to taste the cookies. The young man took a napkin and picked up a cookie, opened his mouth and took a big bite. Oh……. I'll share the rest of the story at the end of the chapter.

The teenage years are a joint venture of conflict, confusion and compassion. Parents trying to find the right combination of reinforcing boundaries and helping kids launch into adulthood can be very difficult.

I remember well the first time we went to the mall and my little girl who was now a teenager no longer wanted to walk near us. Was this the same girl who I used to carry on my shoulders everywhere we went?

We noticed other changes as well around the house. She began to spend more time in her room with the door closed and she wanted to spend more time with her friends and less time with our family. She was changing, and it was as though there was a stranger in our house.

I suppose every generation of adults feels that the next generation offers little reason to be encouraged about the future. This probably comes from the conflict and confusion that is natural between rising teenagers and their mature parents. This is nothing unusual and it happens with every generation.

> *"I see no hope for the future of our people if they are dependent on the frivolous youth of today. For certainly all youth are reckless beyond words. When I was a boy, we were taught to be discreet and*

respectful of elders, but the present youth are exceedingly unwise and impatient." (Greek poet 3000 years ago)

For the last 10 years I have observed the rising generation in this great metropolis (New York City) *and I am convinced that even pagan Rome in its' corrupt age never witnessed more disregard of honor, truth and the common decencies of life."* (R. Sullivan Ives, New York,Times,1864)

"Teenage boys dress like bums and have the manners of

apes." (Hal Boyle –
columnist 1951)

Teenagers are not looking for parents, teachers or youth workers who will dress like them, use all the latest teen vocabulary or mimic their teen lifestyles. They want to be understood, not mimicked. They are looking for mature adults to guide them *in the way they should go*.

Parents and teens tend to pull away from each other during the teenage years. This is normal and part of growing up and becoming more independent.

Parents should do their best to minimize things that cause their teens to pull away from them during the teen years. It would be impossible to identify the many issues, which confront and drive a wedge between parents and teenagers in this short chapter. But most of them can be concentrated in four possible causes.

Parental impatience is one cause of friction between parents and teenagers. Parents must remember that their teenagers still have a great deal to learn. They are not yet adults.

Parents sometimes expect their teenagers to act with maturity and wisdom that they have not yet achieved. Parents tend to judge their teenagers with standards that are unachievable for them. They expect their teens to think, feel, and act in ways and manners as parents might.

Having set those high standards in place, parents become impatient when their teenage children do not rise to the levels they expect from them. Irresponsibility, poor decision-making, and childlike behavior frustrate parents and many times cause them to overreact.

Teenagers struggle with the battle of wanting to grow up, yet wanting the support and security their parents provide. They too are frustrated when they continually fall short of their parents' expectations.

Parents and teenagers should be patient with each other. They should not over expect concerning the behavior of the other or overreact when those expectations are not met.

Keeping lines of communication open between parents and teenagers is of paramount importance. Parents of teenagers must make every effort to talk to one another. This is something both will have to work at.

Parental Insecurity is a second cause of friction between parents and teenagers. Parents sometimes become very insecure when trying to deal with their teenagers.

By the time young people reach their teen years, they have experienced expanding levels of trust and freedom from their parents. They were permitted to go outside the house. They were then permitted to play in the yard but had to stay within the confines of the yard.

When they learned to ride bicycles their borders were expanded even more. Now, in their teenage years, they are looking to see their boundaries expanded even further.

Parents have been used to hands-on control of their children's lives. Now their children are doing the natural thing of wanting more freedom to explore and grow. They are becoming young adults.

The thought of putting their children out there where they could make decisions that could harm them, maybe for the rest of their lives, unnerves parents.

Parents must learn to trust their teenage kids. Parents who have done their best to instill principles of character and right living must trust their children to make right decisions.

In reality, parents have little choice. Their children are growing up and will be confronted with life-impacting decisions, which only they can make.

Parents can address their insecurity. Unity between parents in decision-making and presenting a united front will speak volumes to teenagers.

Parents should carefully consider decisions they make which impact their teenagers. They should take time to explain their reasoning in decisions made to their teenagers.

It is not important that teenagers always agree with their parents, but it is important for teenagers to know their parents have given great thought to the request they have made.

This also will help clearly establish boundaries, which teenagers may not pass.

Teenagers must believe their parents believe in them.

Parental indifference is a third area that creates friction between parents and teenagers. Teenagers and children of all ages are always looking for parental approval and praise.

They may act like they don't want their parents near them. But in reality, they don't want their parents very far away from them.

This may seem like a contradiction and to a certain extent it is. Parents should keep in mind the teenage years are full of contradictions. One-minute children seem to be maturing only to be followed the next minute by childish actions.

Parents must stay engaged with their teenagers. Not in an intrusive sense, but in an interactive sense. Teenagers need to feel their parents are interested in them and what they are doing.

One of the quickest ways to cause distance to develop between parents and teenagers is for parents to be indifferent to the things that are important to the teenagers.

A son may not make the sports team, but he may come home and say he's been asked to serve as the manager of the team.

This is a big deal for him. He is proud of this achievement.

He has been asked to do something important. He's been chosen above others. It's a big deal to him, and it should be a big deal to his parents as well.

The daughter may not have been chosen to head up a special drive at school. But she may have been asked to serve on the planning committee for the drive.

There were only a few students chosen to serve on that committee. This is a big deal to her. She's very proud of her achievement. It's a big deal to her, and it should be a big deal to her parents as well.

Teenagers do not always volunteer information about achievements in their lives. Parents should engage their teenagers in conversation with a discerning ear, listening for clues about things that are important to them.

Parental inconsistency is one the biggest reasons for friction between parents and teenagers. Parents must be consistent in their lifestyles if they expect their teenagers to take them seriously and abide by the requests made of them.

It's hard for teens to take seriously dad's admonition to keep a room clean if mother is always picking up after his dad.

Parents who fail to live consistent lives in front of their teenagers should not be surprised when their teenagers no longer attend church soon after they leave home.

It is important for parents to say the right words, but it's more important for them to live the right way. Their words may fade in the distance, but their consistent lives will ring true through the years.

There are things teenagers desperately need from their parents. Teenagers, in most cases, think they have all the answers.

The problem is they do not know the questions yet that need to be answered in their lives. Parents should recognize how vital it is to equip their teenagers for the future and help them guard their lives in the present.

Accountability, Responsibility, Reward, Loss = *Maturity*

One very important thing teenagers need is **maturity**. How may parents help their teenagers develop maturity?

There are four pillars upon which the house of maturity rests. These are **responsibility, accountability, reward**, and **loss.**

Parents should begin assigning **responsibility** for tasks when children are young. Expectations should be clearly explained. Time frames should be established.

As children grow older, greater levels of responsibility should be given them. Understanding expectations by teenagers and fulfilling those tasks assigned to them will develop a sense of responsibility that will be paramount when they become young adults.

Responsibility should always be followed with **accountability** by parents for their teenagers. Teenagers must know that a time of reckoning will come.

That time of reckoning will require an accounting for the successful completion or failure to complete the responsibility assigned to them.

Responsibility without accountability sends the wrong message to teenagers. They must know that they are responsible to successfully complete tasks assigned to them.

The process of assigning responsibilities, with clearly defined expectations, within specific time frames, with the promise of review and inspection, promotes the maturing process and elevates teenagers' emotional growth.

When teenagers have successfully completed their responsibilities, an appropriate *reward* should be awarded to them. Teenagers learn perseverance and hard work bring rewards.

This is an important lesson for them. Maturity teaches they must successfully complete the task and completed tasks produce rewards.

Teenagers must also learn if they fail to successfully fulfill responsibilities assigned to them, they will suffer *loss*. This is even more important than receiving rewards.

Is important for them to learn that laziness, lack of effort, and just plain being irresponsible comes with a cost. Teens will sometimes test parents' resolve by failing to comply with parents' assignments.

Parents must remain firm and hold them accountable. It must cost their teenagers something when they fail to perform as they should.

A second thing teens need is a measure of ***independence***. Parents should understand that eventually their children are going to grow up, leave home, and build lives away from them.

Preparation for this inevitable event should begin a gradual progression from preschool age through high school.

This independence begins with children learning to use a knife and fork at the dinner table, and continues with permission to play in the front or backyard.

It progresses with permission to occasionally spend the night with a friend at their home. A bicycle expands children's independence to the boundaries of their neighborhoods.

School events, church youth group events, shopping at the mall with a friend, etc., continue to extend their levels of independence.

Parents realize there is a point out there where they must trust their children. They must overcome their own personal insecurities and trust the training they have given and the character of their children.

Violating trust should result in loss for teenagers. Validating trust should be rewarded with greater trust and more independence.

The third thing teenagers' need from their parents is wisdom in **choosing their life's partner**. Moving from adolescence into young adulthood is a trying and difficult time for young people.

Their bodies are changing along with their emotional makeup. Hormones begin to kick in, and teenagers cannot comprehend all that is happening to them.

They are unsure of themselves wanting so badly to be accepted by their peers. They feel awkward in the social graces and a bit inferior to what they view in others as attractive and good-looking.

This is a crucial time for teenagers. Parents need to be aware of their children's needs at this point in their lives.

Teenagers are vulnerable and can be taken advantage of by older and more experienced teenagers. Parents should pay close attention to their teenager's friends. They should note those who may be influencing their teenager in negative ways.

Who teenagers date should matter to their parents. Christian parents should use Biblical principles to advise their teenagers concerning who they should and should not date.

A good passage in the Bible for parents to read and meditate on when advising their teenagers is 2 Corinthians 6:14-16;

> *Be ye not unequally yoked together with unbelievers: for what fellowship hath righteous-ness with unrighteousness? and what communion hath light with darkness? And what concord hath Christ with Belial? or what part hath he that believeth with an infidel? And what agreement hath the temple of God with idols? for ye are the temple of the living God; as God hath said, I will dwell in them,*

*and walk in **them**; and*
I will be their God, and
they shall be my
people.

Mothers should spend time talking with, listening to, and advising their teenage daughters through this difficult time in their lives. They should remind them that they are worth a great deal and not to sell themselves short or devalue themselves.

Fathers should make special efforts in counseling their sons as they approach the dating world. They should remind them how Christian young men should act.

They should also teach them the value of the young ladies they will be dating. These young ladies should be treated with dignity and young men should always act as gentlemen.

Teenagers do not realize how much they need their parents during this time. Parents need to travel the second mile making special efforts to be at the bends in the road in their teenagers need for guidance in this vitally important area of their lives.

A final area in which teenagers need help from their parents is mentoring in **finding their life's vocation**. The Bible says; *Train up a child in the way he should go and when he is old he will not depart from it.*

Unfortunately, this verse is sometimes narrowly interpreted to only include spiritual matters. But the verse is much more powerful than that, and has a deeper meaning as well.

The verse emphasizes the uniqueness of every child. Children are created by God, special and unique with a purpose and plan for their lives.

They possess unique personalities, talents, and abilities. It is important for parents to help these young people discover their uniqueness.

The way the child should go literally means the direction the child should travel in. It's referring to the vocation and occupation that is best suited for them.

They will be their happiest if they find God's intended calling on their lives. Parents should be proactive in encouraging this.

Young people may seem to be floundering when in reality they are simply floating trying to find which way the current of life will carry them.

Parents should make every effort to provide the tools necessary for these young people to find a sense of direction that will lead to the vocation God has in store for them.

Many young people move through high school on their way to college. Parents should be involved with these important and paramount decisions in their teenagers' lives. They should help them see pros and cons and the options of pending decisions they are about to make.

Parent should be careful not to try and live out their own dreams in the lives of the teenagers. They should encourage their teenagers to dream and give them confidence as they reach for their dreams.

The teenage years in most families are times of friction and confusion. Parents and teenagers should take heart; it has always been this way.

Parents have been used to controlling many aspects of their children's lives because they love them and want the very best for them.

Teenagers are ready to expand their horizons, sprout their wings, and soar to heights they have never known before. They will test their wings only to find out the flight can be fledgling at times.

It will come with bumps and bruises but eventually result in leaving the home nest to fly to yet unknown regions beyond their present horizons.

Parents should be proud of their teenagers. They were raised their whole lives for this moment to leap from the mountain top of security at home and fly to regions beyond.

Parents must do all they can to prepare their teenagers to leave the nest. They must believe in the training they have provided, and trust in what their young people have become.

Now back to the oatmeal cookies...

The oatmeal cookies were golden brown and smelled delicious as they cooled on the counter.

The soon-to-be teenager could not resist sampling one. Although it looked good and smelled good, when he bit into it, it tasted horrible.

He could not understand what had gone wrong. He'd followed the directions as best he knew how, yet the cookies didn't turn out the way he imagined they would.

He called the teacher over and tried to describe what was going on. She also tasted the cookies.

She examined the recipe card lying next to the cooling cookies. She began to read the recipe ingredients one by one and the boy nodded his head in compliance with each ingredient.

She came to the soda line of the recipe; it was blurred because of the running ink. She asked the boy; *how much soda did you put in the cookies? 1/2 cup* he replied.

There was a pause in the conversation. His teacher then responded by saying; *the recipe actually calls for 1/2 teaspoon of soda and there is the problem, too much soda.*

Well, this author is that boy. I will always remember what my teacher did next. She said to me:

> *Roy, this is not your fault. You followed the directions but sometimes directions get a little blurred for all of us. When we serve these cookies to the rest of the class, they are going to be special cookies, reserved and not to be touched by anyone. You will receive an A for the cookies.*

I have never forgotten those words spoken to me by my teacher in the seventh grade. It is a reminder of an even greater lesson for parents of teenagers.

Parents may think their instructions in life are very clear to their teenagers. From time to time parts of the recipe for success in life may become a little blurred or skewed in the eyes and understanding of teenagers.

Parents should be careful not to break the spirit of their teenagers by spending too much time on their shortfalls and mistakes.

They should spend more time helping them to become special people because God has something special in life he has reserved for them.

There may seem to be a stranger in the house, but that stranger is not really a stranger at all. Just a teenager on his way to becoming a fine young adult you'll be proud of.

ACTION STEPS

1. What are some things my teenager needs from me as a parent?

_____

_____

_____

_____

2. What are some solid things (pillars) that I can teach my teen that will help him mature and grow up emotionally?

_____

_____

_____

_____

_____

3. What is the most important thing I gained from this chapter?

_____

_____

_____

_____

_____

Chapter 10

Yours, Mine and Ours:
Blended Families 101

The driver of a huge tractor-trailer lost control of his rig and plowed into an empty tollbooth on a busy toll road smashing it to pieces.

He climbed out of the wreckage and within a matter of minutes; a truck pulled up and discharged a crew of workers.

The men picked up each broken piece of the former tollbooth and spread some kind of creamy substance on each one. They began fitting the pieces together.

In less than an hour, they had the entire tollbooth reconstructed and looking good as new.

Astonishing! The truck driver said to the crew chief. *What was the white stuff you used to put all the pieces together?*

At the end of the chapter we'll find out what that magic white stuff was and how it miraculously worked in putting all those pieces back together.

The culture in America continues to change. Statistics tell us that one out of every two marriages will end in divorce. One of the results of the increase in divorce rates is the accelerated growth of blended families.

What is a blended family? According to the dictionary, a blended family is; a *family consisting of a couple and their children from this and all previous relationships*.

One in three weddings in America today form stepfamilies fitting this description, and are considered to be blended families.

As a pastor, educator, and counselor I have worked with many blended family situations over the last 30+ years.

Also, after the death of my first wife I remarried and now am part of a blended family relationship.

There are many resources available beyond the space and restraint of this chapter, which can further aid blended families, who may be struggling to make it work.

"Focus On the Family" posted a great article online titled *Blended Families* written by Natalie Nichols Gillespie. This chapter will lean heavily upon that article as a resource in this chapter.

There are a number of different scenarios, which make up blended families. Each one comes with its own unique set of people, personalities, circumstances, and sometimes conflicts and problems.

Below are five different scenarios along with problems and suggested ways to make each situation hopefully work a little better.

Scenario 1 - *A man with children is left alone because of the death or divorce of his spouse. He meets, dates, falls in love with, and marries another lady. This lady has never been married and has no children of her own.*

Husbands and wives often move into this relationship with different expectations. Husbands often make the mistake of assuming that their new wives will fill the same role as their previous wife. They expect them to not only be their wives, but to also become instant mothers to their children.

The new bride on the other hand has never been married before. She is looking for romance and building a relationship with her new husband. Quality time as a couple is what she wants and needs.

The role of wife is totally new to her. Being asked to become an instant mom can become overwhelming to her.

Wives often feel frustrated, disillusioned, and lost when they are given the responsibility of caring for someone else's children. Many times the children resent this also.

The husband should understand the necessity of building this new relationship with his wife first. He must allow her time to adjust to their marital relationship.

He must work at making her feel special and providing the security that she needs in the marriage.

Disciplining the children should primarily be his responsibility at the beginning of the marriage. He should do this to avoid conflicts between his new bride and his children.

Children should learn from fathers to treat their stepmothers with respect and dignity. Her role with the children and her responsibilities in the home along with their responsibilities should be clearly defined for all to understand.

It will take time for her to gain their respect and confidence of the children. She will have to earn this one-day-at-a-time.

Scenario 2 - *A woman with children is left alone because of the death or divorce of her spouse. She meets, falls in love with, and marries another man. This man has never been married and has no children of his own.*

Women, who are left to raise children on their own, find themselves in a very difficult situation. Providing for the material and emotional needs of their children can be difficult and emotionally draining.

Women often make the mistake of seeing a new husband as an answer to ease the load they have been carrying.

If wives shift too many responsibilities concerning the children to their new husbands, rebellion and conflict may be the result. The children believe they have a dad and don't need another one.

Stepfathers should tread softly in administering discipline. The biological parents should make the rules and handle the discipline initially.

It will take time for newly married couples to develop a solid front to the children. This will happen when they take time to develop the relationship and bond together.

Wives should be careful not to neglect and shut out their husbands in favor of the children.

Talking about the husband or engaging in conversations with the children about events and situations the husband has no knowledge of will make him feel left out and less a part of the family.

There is a fine line between handling discipline and devaluing the husband's position in the home.

Putting down the husband in front of the children will undercut his authority and may cause the children to disregard and even disrespect him.

Children will not be forced to love their new stepparent. The wise mother will recognize this and instead work towards establishing respect by her children for their stepfather.

Children should be required to show the

same respect for their new stepdad as they would for their teachers, law enforcement officers, and anyone else in positions of authority.

Scenario 3 - *A divorced man or woman with children marries another divorced man or woman who also has children.*

This scenario is probably one of the hardest to work through in the beginning of the new relationship. But it has great potential for being successful. Mom and dad are both motivated to make every effort to pull the kids together in their new family.

This blended family may be the most difficult for the children. Children experience a loss when their biological parent marries someone who also has children.

Now they have to share their biological parent with not only their new spouse but also the new spouse's children.

Their space in the home is shared with a new parent and now stepsiblings. They may move to a new city, live in a new home, transfer to a new school, and maybe even have a new roommate in their new blended family.

Couples who are divorced and remarried must remember their children love both them and their other biological parent.

When the new family is formed, it effectively kills the dream, which many children hold dear that their biological parents will eventually get back together again.

Studies show the first two years of all stepfamilies are transition years and very crucial in the long-term success of these families.

Families should expect conflict and be willing to compromise, show compassion, understanding, and grace to their new family members.

There will be a variety of relationships between members of this type of stepfamily, different levels of intimacy, connection, and love between stepsiblings and between children and stepparents. They can make this work. But if it is to be successful, it will require hard work.

Scenario 4 - *A spouse dies leaving the mate to raise the children. The mate falls in love and remarries bringing a new spouse into the home.*

Losing a spouse or parent leaves a grieving household. One spouse remarries and brings someone new into the home; inevitably memories of the family member who has passed will arise.

The new stepparent or spouse should be aware of this and know they will be confronted with it at some point.

Grieving will sometimes continue for years. Stepfamilies should take important steps in order to heal from their grief so they can build happy and united new families.

The role of stepparents in this situation is to become a friend and mentor to the children. They should not assume the role as a parent because the children are not ready for their parent to be replaced.

Families should not shy away from honoring the loved one who's passed on with photographs and memories. But care should be taken not to erect monuments or shrines to idolize the dead family member.

It is important to create environments that will allow growth and intimacy between the spouses and also between children and their parents.

The way to do this is to create a level playing field by establishing common ground so stepparents and stepchildren can move forward together. This is not easy, but it can be done.

Scenario 5 - *The children have grown up and their widowed or divorced parents decide to remarry.*

I have personal knowledge of this scenario. I was a widower with grown married children when I remarried. Widowed couples that remarry are still considered stepfamilies.

Connecting and bonding between grown children and a newly introduced spouse is more difficult because they do not have the daily interactions like children who live in the home.

Relationships can be strained for years and may never reach any level of real intimacy.

Fears over future inheritance, sentimental family objects etc., sometimes create friction between biological parents and their spouses with the grown children.

A number of proactive things can be done to alleviate fears and be inclusive with the children in the decision-making process.

Communication between biological parents and their grown children beginning with the widowed parent's dating relationships, can make a huge difference.

Children should be informed well in advance of an impending marriage of their parents. Springing a last-minute wedding raises red flags to adult grown children.

Including children in the loop makes them feel that they are valuable in their parents' eyes and that their feelings are important.

Establishing what sentimental things are important to the children and then distributing those things to the children is also important.

A daughter seeing her dad's new wife wearing her mom's jewelry can be devastating.

A son seeing his mom's new husband brandishing one of his father's favorite guns can make him angry.

By giving the daughter or daughters their choice on the jewelry, and giving the son or sons their favorite gun or tool announces to them that they are still important to their mom or dad.

Letting the children know their inheritance is secure and that they and the new spouse will all be treated fairly will help pave the way towards developing growing, healthy relationships.

The widowed spouse should seek to create a new place for his spouse in the hearts of the children and grandchildren. That place occupied by the deceased spouse will always be special to the children and grandchildren.

If the widowed spouse will handle it well, they will gladly open their hearts and create another special place for the new stepparent.

No matter what type of stepfamily yours may be, with the right resources and the help of God, family, and friends, your stepfamily can find encouragement and hope.

Now Back to Our Story.........

When the driver of a huge trailer lost control of his rig, he plowed into an empty tollbooth and smashed it to pieces.

He climbed down from the wreckage and within a matter of minutes; a truck pulled up and discharged a crew of workers.

The men picked up each broken piece of the former tollbooth and spread some kind of creamy substance on each one. They began fitting the pieces together.

In less than an hour, they had the entire tollbooth reconstructed and looking good as new.

Astonishing! The truck driver said to the crew chief. *What was the white stuff you used to get all the pieces together*?

The crew chief said, *Oh that was tollgate booth paste*.

I know, you are thinking *what a corny story.* I guess I would agree but I think there is a great truth in the story.

Many families seem to pass through times like the tollbooth. Everything seems to be going well then out of nowhere something comes along like death or divorce and smashes everything into pieces.

We hope and pray that somehow it can all be put back together again. But at some point we realize there is no *magic glue* that can ever make it the way it was before.

Then something totally unexpected happens. God comes along and helps us build a new family. It is not exactly like the one we had before, but never the less it is a family that God has put together for us.

We will have to try hard, do our best to understand others and make some compromises, some personal changes, but it will be worth it. With God's help we can enjoy our new families.

ACTION STEPS

1. Which scenario best describes your family?

_____

_____

_____

_____

2. What is the biggest problem facing my blended family?

_____

_____

_____

_____

_____

3. What can I take from this chapter that will help my family?

_____

_____

_____

_____

Chapter 11

Parenting My

Adult Children

Roy's son Aaron and his family from left to right: Claire, Aaron, Susan, Lauren, and Rachel.

Ephesians 6:1-3

Children, obey your parents in the Lord, for this is right. Honor your father and mother (which is the first commandment with a promise), so that it may be well with you, and that you may live long on the earth.

What is one of the basic tenets, which binds parents with their children? How does that bond hold true throughout the rest of their lives?

Children must be taught early to *respect* their parents. *Respect* is something that is not only talked but must be earned by parents.

How do children learn to respect their parents? There are two very important things that children must learn in order to properly respect their parents. The first one normally leads to the second.

How long should a child be considered a child? Failure to have a clear understanding of this important clarification will create friction and cause conflicts between parents and children.

Unfortunately, many young adults wish to continue to receive material support and finances from their parents but do not want their parents to have a voice in the way they live their lives, and spend their money.

How long should a child be considered a child? A child is considered a child as long as he receives room, board, insurance, and financial support from his parents. As long as he depends on his parents for substance and support is another way of saying it.

When are children not considered to be children anymore? A child is no longer considered a child when he makes his own living and takes care of his own expenses without help from his parents.

1. The Relationship Between Parents and Grown children who choose to remain in their parents' homes

I remember from my teenage years a statement made by my father. I was sprouting my wings, testing the headwaters of authority in the home, and would soon be on my own. I pushed my father too far one day.

My father said to me; *as long as you put your feet under my table and sleep between my sheets you'll do what I say in this house.* My father clearly defined the relationship and boundaries between himself and me.

This area is very important today because of the shift in the American culture of young adults aged 18 to 29 who are still living at home with their parents. The March 2012 Pew Research Center tabulations taken from the Current Population Survey (CPS) graph below indicate that one in three young adults

(36%) between 18 and 31 are still living at home with their parents.

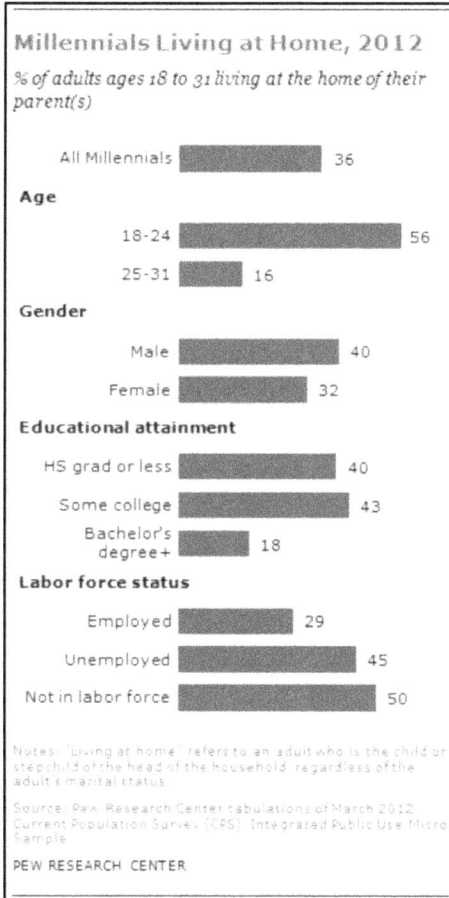

Millennials Living at Home, 2012

% of adults ages 18 to 31 living at the home of their parent(s)

All Millennials	36
Age	
18-24	56
25-31	16
Gender	
Male	40
Female	32
Educational attainment	
HS grad or less	40
Some college	43
Bachelor's degree+	18
Labor force status	
Employed	29
Unemployed	45
Not in labor force	50

Notes: "Living at home" refers to an adult who is the child or stepchild of the head of the household, regardless of the adult's marital status.

Source: Pew Research Center tabulations of March 2012 Current Population Survey (CPS) Integrated Public Use Micro Sample

PEW RESEARCH CENTER

There may be legitimate reasons why Millennials remain in their parents' homes after high school and/or college. Whatever these reasons may be, parents should remember their children have become grown up adults. Their children have reached the ages in life when they normally should be out on their own.

Our culture today is producing children of entitlement. The *every child gets a trophy syndrome* makes no distinction between winning and losing.

We must encourage our children but we must be careful not to instill in them a misunderstanding of how life works. The world tells us that the more material possessions and things that we provide for our children the better parents we are.

This is a totally false precept upon which to attempt to build character in our children. Children grow up expecting more and more from parents and the society in which they live. They become young adults and remain in the home expecting their parents to continue to give them more and more.

Young adult children who remain at home with their parents should not be treated in the same fashion as when they were much younger. It would be wise for parents to sit down with their grown children who remain in their homes, and come to an understanding of how the arrangement will work.

Parents should define the roles in this developing relationship. They should clearly define what is expected of their grown children remaining in the home.

The main goal of both parents and children should be the ultimate self-support of the child outside the home. Parents should help their children work toward that end.

Parents should insist that grown children remaining in the home seek employment. In other words, they must get a job. Children must actively be seeking and eventually secure a means of income.

Parents should also insist and offer assistance in developing a budget with their children that will aid them in reaching the goal of self-sufficiency.

Children should help pay for their keep. Food and utilities cost the parents money. An extra adult in the house increases water, electricity, and food expenses.

Grown children should pay a reasonable agreed-upon amount at regular intervals, such as weekly or monthly to help their parents with expenses. They should do this not only to help their parents, but as a means of self-respect for themselves.

Grown children should be responsible for keeping their rooms clean and doing their own laundry. They should help with family related tasks around the home.

Setting the table, clearing the table, washing dishes and putting them away, helps ease Mom's burdens and responsibilities.

Young men should help with cutting the grass; taking the garbage can to the curb, and looking for ways to help ease Dad's burdens and responsibilities as well.

Young adults remaining in the home should be responsible for their personal items.

Hair-care products, deodorant, perfume, cologne, aftershave, shaving cream, razors, clothing, snacks and on and on are the responsibility of grown children. They should not expect nor should parents provide these items for them.

Young adults should be responsible for car payments, car insurance, car maintenance, and gasoline for their cars. Parents should not finance these things for their children.

Parents should also be very careful about *cosigning for car payments*. Young adults are attracted to flashy new cars, which sometimes they cannot afford. Parents end up making payments on vehicles for their children that are newer and better than their own.

2. The Relationship Between Parents and Grown Children after the Children Leave Home.

Should children always obey their parents? Is there a difference between the obligation to obey parents and to honor them?

Should parents aid their grown children financially after they've left home and are on their own?

Should parents have input in their grown children's personal and family lives?

The relationship between parents and their grown children must change of necessity once children leave home and are on their own.

One great tenet of parental responsibility is preparing their children to grow up, make a living, create their own families, and make it in their own world.

So, are children obligated to always obey their parents? While children are living under their parents' roofs, receiving the benefits of their parents' material wealth and relying upon their parents' assets to meet their needs, they are obligated to obey their parents' wishes.

The relationship between parents and grown children changes when children declare their independence by leaving home and supporting themselves.

When children reach the point in their lives that they can take care of themselves, they are no longer obligated to obey their parents.

Parents should respect this point in their children's lives and treat them like adults.

Parents should not intrude into the personal and family lives of their grown children.

They must allow their children to make their own decisions even if those decisions might not be the ones the parents would've made.

Children will make mistakes. They may not always make the best decisions. But they must learn, just as their parents learned, and this takes time and experience.

Should parents provide financial support for their grown children after they leave home? The short answer to this question is yes if they choose to.

Parents are under no obligation to give their grown children money once they leave home and are on their own. Circumstances may arise when parents feel impressed to offer a financial helping hand to their children.

Finding the delicate balance between caution and generosity can sometimes be difficult for parents. Parents should not rush in every time their children have a financial crisis.

Sometimes there is financial pain that comes with making bad decisions. Children should feel this pain in order to learn how to make better decisions.

Parents who become their children's banks will cause their children to become financially challenged. Their children will never learn how to manage their money, take care of their families and improve their lifestyles. They will remain financially anemic in a world that demands much more.

Children who are working hard, managing their money well in doing the very best they know how occasionally may hit a bump in the road financially. Those children should know that mom and dad would be there in cases of calamity or financial emergencies.

They understand that Mom and Dad are not their banks but Mom and Dad love them and would never want them to go without the basic necessities of life.

Children who are doing their best to take care of themselves and their families rarely seek financial assistance from their parents. It is a very difficult thing for them to come to their parents in times of need.

But one thing is certain; the request will be an exception and not a habit.

When parents provide financial assistance to their grown children, they have a right to know the circumstances of the need and how the money they provide will be spent.

Children, who are not willing to talk over the details of the situation, are not appreciative of what their parents are about to do, and those children should not receive financial support from their parents.

3. Grown Children Have the Responsibility to HONOR Their Parents.

The Greek word for *HONOR* means to value, revere or prize. Honoring our parents is showing respect in what we say and how we treat them. This treatment comes from an attitude of appreciating the position they hold and the merit they have earned.

One of the Ten Commandments in Exodus 20:12 makes it clear that children of all ages have a responsibility to honor their parents;

> *Honor your father and your mother, so that your days may be long upon the land which the LORD your God gives you.*

The New Testament reinforces this in

Ephesians 6:1-3;

> *Children, obey your parents in the Lord, for this is right. Honor your father and mother, which is the first commandment with a promise, so that it may be well with you, and that you may live long on the earth.*

Children should honor their parents with their thoughts, words, and actions in much the same way they bring glory to God.

They should respect the authority of their parents by listening, and heeding, when possible, to their parents' requests and wishes.

Even if they do not agree with their parents, they should be respectful in listening to and considering what their parents say.

God will honor children who honor their parents. Honoring parents is not always easy and sometimes not possible in our own strength.

But honoring our parents is not optional. Colossians 3:20 reminds us;

> *Children, obey your*
> *parents in all things, for*
> *this is well pleasing to*
> *the Lord.*

Roy's daughter Missy and her family, from left to right: Mason, Missy, Tim and Marissa.

ACTION STEPS

1. What are specific problems am I facing in my relationship with my family?

_____

_____

_____

_____

2. What one thing comes to mind that will help me with my family relationship?

_____

_____

_____

_____

3. What is the most valuable thing I

learned from this chapter?

_____

_____

_____

_____

Dr. Harris is in high demand as Conference and Retreat Speaker. He has spoken in 38 American States, Europe, Israel and Africa ministering in over 400 business organizations, schools, colleges and churches.

Roy began ***Roy Harris Ministries*** in 2007 as a ministry to help and encourage pastors, churches, Christian educators and Christian businesses.

Roy Harris Ministries has grown into a multifaceted ministry including but not limited to:
Living Beyond Grief Conferences
Pastor/Staff Leadership Conferences
Church Renewal Conferences
Church Evangelism Conferences
Couples Retreats
Men's Retreats
Family Enrichment Days
Traditional Church Revival Meetings

Go online www.royharris.info for more information on each of these and much more about Roy and how he might help your church, school, or business.

For more information contact Dr. Harris:

roy@royharris.info
(615-351-1425)
906 Castle Heights Ave
Lebanon, TN 37087

Another book by Dr. Harris

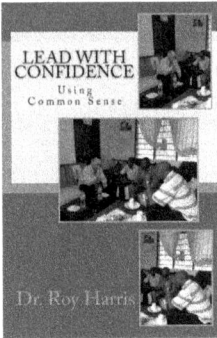

LEAD with CONFIDENCE is a unique and practical book every leader will want on his shelf. The book offers a common sense approach to making hard decisions, relationship building, communication, delegating responsibility, receiving and giving criticism, correcting and disciplining others, second guessing past decisions, leadership discernment, conducting business meetings, managing time wisely and much more.

The book contains an added bonus; a helpful *STUDY GUIDE* conveniently located at the end of each chapter.

Purchase your copy.

@

www.Amazon.com)

or send $15.00 for each copy (includes shipping) to:

LEAD with CONFIDENCE
906 Castle Heights Ave
Lebanon, TN 37087
For more Information e-mail or call Roy
Roy @royharris.info **615-351-1425**.

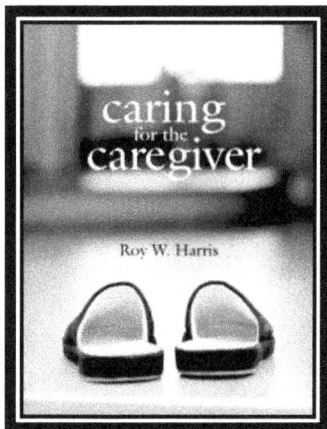

A book by Roy for those providing care to the terminally ill. For three years Roy provided loving care for his terminally ill wife Diana until her death. He wrote the book to encourage and help those who provide care to terminally ill loved ones and friends and also to help others better understand how to encourage and help caregivers.

What others have said...

"As a caregiver myself (my wife has MS), I was moved, encouraged, helped, comforted, challenged, and blessed. You will be, too." **Robert Morgan,** Senior Pastor, The Donelson Fellowship - Nashville, TN

"This book is a must for every caregiver, pastor, deacon, choir director, youth worker, health care worker, and anyone who wants to better understand how to help and encourage caregivers. Thanks Roy…. Many people will be helped and encouraged by this book." **Stan Toler,** Church of the Nazarene.

Copies of the book may be ordered online at www.amazon.com. For an autographed copy send a check for $13.00 (includes shipping) to:

Caring for the Caregiver
Roy Harris
906 Castle Heights Ave.
Lebanon, TN 37087

www.ingramcontent.com/pod-product-compliance
Lightning Source LLC
Chambersburg PA
CBHW071955040426
42447CB00009B/1349